Teaching History Online

Bringing history teaching into the twenty-first century, *Teaching History Online* is a concise guide to developing and using internet resources in history instruction. It offers practical, jargon-free advice to help the history teacher develop online assignments, and provides an informed introduction to the myriad resources and tools available for use in the online classroom.

Beginning with a chapter on the benefits of teaching and studying online, John F. Lyons goes on to address instructors' most commonly asked questions and concerns, including:

- designing an online class;
- providing online alternatives to the lecture;
- developing a user-friendly discussion board;
- conducting assessment;
- dealing with classroom management.

For historians interested in providing an online element to their traditional face-to-face classroom teaching, the final chapter shows how to develop successful hybrid/blended classes.

An accessible introduction and valuable resource, *Teaching History Online* includes sample lesson plans, examples of online learning tools, and suggestions for further reading, helping those who use – or want to use – online resources to create exciting, interactive and rewarding learning environments.

John F. Lyons is associate professor of history at Joliet Junior College in Illinois where he teaches British history, US history, world history, and Latin American history. His publications include *Teachers and Reform: Chicago Public Education, 1929–70* (2008).

Student/instructor resources at the companion website: www.routledge.com/textbooks/9780415482226.

Teaching History Online

John F. Lyons

Routledge
Taylor & Francis Group

LONDON AND NEW YORK

First published 2009
by Routledge
2 Park Square, Milton Park, Abingdon, Oxon OX14 4RN

Simultaneously published in the USA and Canada
by Routledge
270 Madison Ave, New York, NY 10016

Routledge is an imprint of the Taylor & Francis Group, an informa business

© 2009 John F. Lyons

Typeset in Bell Gothic by
Florence Production Ltd, Stoodleigh, Devon
Printed and bound in Great Britain by
TJ International Ltd, Padstow, Cornwall

British Library Cataloguing in Publication Data
A catalogue record for this book is available from the British Library

Library of Congress Cataloging in Publication Data
Lyons, John F., 1960–.
   Teaching history online/John F. Lyons.
      p. cm.
   Includes bibliographical references and index.
   1. History—Web-based instruction.   I. Title.
   D16.255.C65L962008
   907.85′4678—dc22   2008027945

ISBN10: 0–415–48221–6 (hbk)
ISBN10: 0–415–48222–4 (pbk)
ISBN10: 0–203–88424–8 (ebk)

ISBN13: 978–0–415–48221–9 (hbk)
ISBN13: 978–0–415–48222–6 (pbk)
ISBN13: 978–0–203–88424–9 (ebk)

To Joanie and Sinead

Contents

Illustrations

Figures

Tables

Acknowledgments

A number of people have been instrumental in helping me bring this book to fruition. I'd like to thank the Faculty Development Committee at Joliet Junior College for providing me with a sabbatical to write the book and the wonderful library staff at the college for fulfilling my often esoteric requests. I'd like to thank Marti Bonne, Laura Jo Cashmer, Julie Havemann and Bill Yarrow for providing insightful comments on draft chapters of the book. Thanks to my fellow instructors from Joliet Junior College who participated in the Master Online Teacher Certificate program at the University of Illinois Global Campus in 2006 and 2007 for sharing with me their own experiences of teaching online. I learned much about the technology and the pedagogy of teaching online from conversations with Jane Cartwright, Chris Harvey and Jeff Nuckles in the Distance Education department. My students helped me to revaluate my teaching by offering astute feedback on all of my courses.

The publication of this book depended on a number of collaborators. I'd like to thank Eve Setch for showing enthusiasm for this project from the beginning, and Gerry Herman and the other readers at Routledge for providing thoughtful suggestions for revision. They helped me clarify my thoughts and greatly improved the quality of the book. Thanks also to Alison Yates and Amanda Crook for making the production process run so smoothly. The screenshots, which were taken from my online courses, and the commonly asked questions section were reproduced with the kind permission of Joliet Junior College. Parts of Chapters 1, 3 and 5 have been taken from "Teaching US History Online: Problems and Prospects," published in *The History Teacher* 37 (August 2004): 447–56, and has been reproduced with the kind permission of Jane Dabel, Editor, *The History Teacher*.

My extended family has nurtured the creation of the book. Dad, Mike and Mary supplied encouragement and humor from England, while Dorothy, Mike and Eddie offered the same from closer to home. I'd like to thank my daughter Sinead for brightening up every day and for allowing her dad to write the book by napping during the afternoons and going to bed early. Michele, Enrico and Giorgia provided friendship and stepped in at crucial stages by taking Sinead to their house or to the park. Finally, I'd like to thank Joanie for providing me with love, sunshine and unwavering support.

Why teach and study online?

C OMPUTER-MEDIATED ONLINE COURSES are increasingly becoming an accepted part of college and high-school teaching. All across the world, institutions of higher education are offering online courses to students at home and abroad. In 2003 1.98 million college students enrolled in online classes in the United States; a 22.9 percent increase over the previous year. In 2004 the number grew another 18.2 percent to reach 2.35 million. By 2005 the figure had climbed to nearly 3.2 million students. In 2006, nearly 20 percent of enrollment in postsecondary institutions in the US was in online classes.[1] The Open University, the leading distance education institution based in the UK, has seen its enrollment increase by nearly a third from 170,000 students in 1998–9 to 220,000 in 2005–6.[2] In a survey of 150 European educational institutions undertaken in 2005, three-quarters believed that "computer-based learning had a major role in most of their courses or would do so within three years."[3] Schools have also increasingly added online classes to their course offerings. Enrollment in US pre-collegiate online courses has grown from 50,000 students in 2000 to about 1 million in 2006. In April 2006 Michigan became the first state in the US to require high-school students to take an online course before they graduate.[4]

It is easy to see why online classes are so popular with students. Shift workers, frequent travelers, those who find it difficult to attend college because of physical disabilities or because they live in rural areas, and parents who want to spend more time at home with their children can all take advantage of the flexible schedules offered by online classes. Some students simply prefer to work alone and at their own pace rather than attend a traditional face-to-face class. Shy students who dread the traditional classroom or those who are embarrassed by their underdeveloped language skills may also prefer the anonymity of the online environment. A new generation of students, more comfortable with technology because of their experience of using social networking sites such as MySpace and Facebook, downloading music from the Internet, communicating with cell phones and playing video games, seem to want to engage with computer technology in their learning.

Online classes present many advantages to both instructors and the college administration too. Online teaching offers instructors the choice to teach from home as well as from college or to teach even when the instructor is out of town, or out of the country, attending a conference or undertaking a research trip. Costly and time-consuming commutes and looking for parking spaces on crowded campuses can be ended. Teaching online also means less time spent photocopying class handouts and an end to setting up overhead projectors, PowerPoint presentations, and video viewings in the classroom. Educational institutions are able to attract the tuition of working students as government funds for education are limited. Student enrollment can increase without the necessity of building more classrooms, student accommodation on campus, and parking lots.

More than simply providing convenience for students, instructors and colleges, online technology offers enormous educational benefits as it fosters and enhances student-centered learning. Educational research suggests that the model of teaching too often found in the traditional face-to-face classroom, which emphasizes the transfer of information from teachers to students by lecturing, needs to be replaced by a more learner-centered approach. Collaborative learning, students pursuing their own interests, and peer review are important components of student-centered learning. Online technology, which extends learning beyond the time and space constraints of the traditional classroom, makes it easier to adopt a student-centered approach. Online learning offers a range of content such as websites, audio, simulations, videos, text and other multimedia resources to reach all learning styles. Discussion boards, blogs and wikis facilitate social learning and can engage students more than a classroom lecture. The world of the Internet provides students with other avenues to obtain information than just relying on the instructor.

Although the number of classes offered online has proliferated, many instructors express concern about teaching distance education courses. One history professor who conducted a comparative study of his distance and traditional courses reported that "use of the Internet and multimedia projects negatively affected student interest, communication with the instructor, and performance."[5] Many professors informed *The Chronicle of Higher Education* that they used technology in the traditional face-to-face class but would not teach online because they disliked the lack of social interaction.[6] Other instructors complain that answering emails and participating in discussion boards mean that online teaching takes up more of their time than a traditional class.[7] One online instructor criticized the "attitudes and behaviors" of online students who did not take assignment deadlines seriously, expected instantaneous feedback from the instructor, and often sent rude emails to the teacher and to the student discussion board. "The reality of online teaching can be confounding and upsetting. It can make a talented teacher feel like an unmitigated failure," she concluded.[8]

Although problems such as those mentioned above are a concern, it is still possible to create an online learning experience that is rewarding for both the teacher and the students. To accomplish this, an instructor needs to possess a certain amount of technical knowledge, but more than anything instructors require good teaching skills, not technical know-how, to achieve success in an online class. Indeed, a teacher in an online class needs to possess many of the same skills as a teacher in a traditional classroom. Instructors must have a sound knowledge of their subject matter, a passion for teaching, good organizational skills, a caring attitude to their students and high expectations of those they teach.

The purpose of this book is to assist instructors in translating their teaching skills to the online environment. This book will guide instructors through the process of designing and teaching an online class by addressing their most frequently asked questions and concerns. Although *Teaching History Online* is based on the most up-to-date educational research and theoretical ideas, the focus is on the practice rather than the theory of teaching. My views of teaching history online is gained from reflection on my own online teaching experiences, extensive reading of the theoretical and research literature on online learning, and discussions with online practitioners, both instructors and students. The book includes tried and tested instructional methods, ideas for assignments and assessment, examples of exemplary Web-based learning tools and online history resources, and guides to further reading. At some points in the book, I've prescribed a single teaching strategy based on my own teaching experience; at other times I lay out the advantages and disadvantages of various strategies, allowing instructors to make choices based on their own teaching style.

If all online instructors need strong teaching skills, why do we need an online book that is devoted solely to history? There are many guides that claim to help teachers develop computer-mediated online classes, but most are not discipline specific and offer no practical advice to history teachers. Yet each subject requires different teaching techniques, tools, and resources to produce a successful learning experience. The Internet and computer technology provides students with access to a wide range of tools and resources that offer almost limitless possibilities for undertaking historical inquiry. Indeed, the objective of history teaching, allowing students to construct historical arguments using primary and secondary sources, is made easier in the online environment. *Teaching History Online* provides instructors with concrete information about online tools and resources and some examples of assignments to help those teaching history online.

Teaching History Online is divided into six main chapters. Chapter 1 helps instructors to begin designing an online class, and Chapter 2 provides online alternatives to the classroom lecture. Because the discussion board is so important and popular in an online class, the whole of Chapter 3 is devoted to online discussions. The fourth chapter looks at the many different ways online instructors may assess students, and Chapter 5 is devoted to classroom management issues. Online learning is changing how we can teach face-to-face classes. Therefore, the final chapter offers suggestions to instructors who teach hybrid/blended classes and to those who want to incorporate online elements into the traditional face-to-face classroom. The book cannot cover every facet of online teaching, so at the end of each chapter I have included a list of further readings. The lists are not definitive, but these resources will provide deeper insights into online learning and help the online instructor to broaden their knowledge. At the end of the book, the reader will find a number of appendices containing course rubrics, a syllabus, a website review assignment, a consent form for an oral history project and a student course evaluation form. Like all the other information in this book, instructors should feel free to adapt these to suit their own teaching style.

Chapter 1

Getting started

T0 DESIGN A HISTORY COURSE, for both the online and the traditional face-to-face classroom, requires an enormous amount of work. The
subject of the course must be thoroughly mastered, readings chosen, course
lectures written, assignments developed and a syllabus produced. Compared to
traditional courses, however, online classes require far more of the instructor's
time in preparation. Those teaching in the traditional classroom can change
their assignments and lectures the night before class, but the online curriculum
cannot be altered at such short notice. Before the class even begins, the
instructor must design and construct an online site that contains all the course
elements for the whole semester. To design an online class, instructors require
a knowledge of how students learn, ought to master the basics of using a course
management system, should obtain some critical information about the students
they teach, need to understand the challenges of online teaching, and must
envision the goals of the course.

Intellectual property rights

As soon as a college or school approaches an instructor to teach an online class,
intellectual property rights need to be firmly established. Who owns the online
course site the instructor creates? Can an instructor produce a site and then see
the college employ someone else to use it? Both the instructor and the college
have legitimate rights to the course. The instructor creates the course, but he
or she also receives a salary, and uses employer resources, to develop it.
Because of this, an instructor, or their union, ought to negotiate an intellectual
property agreement with their college administrators. Some such agreements
assign ownership to instructors even if they've used college resources to develop
the course. Others allocate full ownership of online courses to the college, not
the creator of the course. Many institutions that claim ownership of online

courses now offer the creating instructor "rights of first refusal" with respect both to revision and teaching of the course. Another option is joint ownership of the online course between the instructor and the college. If the instructor moves to another college, he or she can continue to use the course materials. At the same time, the college retains the right to offer the course with a different instructor if the creator of the course is not available or not willing to teach it.

The basics of teaching and learning

To create and teach an online course, instructors must first understand how students learn. The thousands of articles and books produced on student learning may disagree on the finer points but all lead towards the same conclusion: students must be active, rather than passive, in their learning. According to a number of studies, students remember 90 percent of what they do, 50 percent of what they see, but only 10 percent of what they hear. Therefore, instructors need to be creative to make assignments that rely less on students passively listening to lectures and more on engaging students in independent discovery. In this regard, online history students need to undertake writing, problem solving, role playing, discussion, analysis of primary sources and other active learning assignments to acquire a real understanding of history.

The learning theory of constructivism points towards a number of teaching practices in the online environment. Constructivists believe that learners understand new material through the interaction of prior experiences or beliefs with new ideas. Constructivists tell us to relate course topics and assignments to the students' own lives and to their existing knowledge. Students pursue their own interests and research, rather than have instructors narrowly confine them to a set curriculum of readings and assignments. Open-ended questioning and real-world problem solving are part of the constructivist classroom. Writing journals, portfolios and class presentations replaces factual quizzes as forms of assessment. In the history classroom, constructivist theory suggests that there are different perspectives and that findings are open to interpretation and debate. Primary source documents are the center of the history classroom as students act like real historians sifting through contradictory interpretations. Just as important, students use their own experiences and understanding of life to partake in role playing or simulation exercises.

Active learning and constructivism are essential in any history course because they help students develop critical thinking and higher forms of understanding. Benjamin Bloom's famous *Taxonomy of Educational Objectives*, published in 1956, established a hierarchy of educational objectives ranging from the simple recall of facts to synthesis and evaluation (see Table 1.1). Instructors need to spend more time on activities and assessments that encourage

Table 1.1 Benjamin Bloom's *Taxonomy of Educational Objectives*

Category	Meaning
Evaluation	Make judgments
Synthesis	Create from different sources
Analysis	Make inferences
Application	Use a concept in a new situation
Comprehension	Understand and put in one's own words
Knowledge	Recall information

higher-level thinking skills rather than lower-level ones. At the end of the semester, students should be able not only to identify the main figures and events in history but also to evaluate different forms of evidence and sources, and demonstrate an ability to undertake original historical research.

Many educational studies have also concluded that cooperative learning should be a major component of college teaching. In a cooperative learning environment, students learn by collaboratively working on assignments and projects and participating in small group discussions, which provides them with opportunities to share their ideas and to learn from each other. In the process, students engage in rigorous debate but learn to show consideration and respect for the opinions of others. Cooperative learning, increasingly used in the traditional face-to-face classroom, can also be adapted to the online environment. For example, students can contribute to online discussion boards and work in small groups using online communication tools.

If active learning, constructivism and cooperative learning should be important elements of any online history class, instructors should also be aware that students have different styles of learning and different interests. Howard Gardner's ideas on multiple intelligences are a good starting point from which to think about the different assignments we can use online. Gardner identifies at least eight different kinds of learning styles: linguistic, logical-mathematical, spatial, bodily kinesthetic, musical, interpersonal, intrapersonal and naturalist. It is possible to design an online class that can reach the various learning intelligences of all the students. For instance, reading and writing would interest the linguistic learner. Quantitative history would appeal to logical-mathematical learners. Assignments that include photos, paintings and videos would appeal to the spatial learner. Interactive technology and simulations would help bodily kinesthetic learners. Musical learners would be addressed by including assignments with music. Discussion boards and a group project would permit interpersonal learners to interact with other students. For the introverted intrapersonal learner, a self-reflective journal activity would meet the requirements

Table 1.2 Multiple intelligences

Category	Meaning	Online Activity
Linguistic	Ability to use words, spoken or written	Compose essays and journals, read books, diaries and letters, and produce podcasts
Logical-Mathematical	Ability with numbers and reasoning	Analyze and produce historical statistical data, charts and timelines
Spatial	Ability with images	View and produce paintings, posters, photographs and videos
Bodily-Kinesthetic	Ability to use bodily movement	Participate in simulations and role playing, and visit historical sites
Musical	Ability with rhythm and music	Analyze songs and lyrics, and produce presentations with music
Interpersonal	Ability to interact with others	Participate in cooperative learning, group work, and the discussion board
Intrapersonal	Ability to work alone and self-reflect	Write journals and essays
Naturalist	Ability to recognize patterns in nature	Analyze maps, battle field simulations and environmental history

while the naturalist learner would enjoy assignments involving maps and environmental history. Resources available online make it possible to accommodate all learning styles (see Table 1.2).

What all this tells us is that we should provide varied forms of learning activities and teaching strategies in our online classes. Online instructors ought to design a course that focuses on active learning, higher-level thinking, and collaboration with others. Instructors need to develop assignments that reach all learning styles and provide course material in a variety of forms using written text, audio, and visuals. At the same time, instructors should take into account diverse student interests and allow students to choose their own assessments or assignments as much as possible.

Course management systems

Most educational institutions now use course management systems (CMSs) (also called learning management systems or virtual learning environments) to help instructors create online courses. There are many CMSs, such as ANGEL, Blackboard, eCollege and Moodle, that provide online shells into which instructors add their course content. CMSs vary in appearance and in features but have some common elements. They offer students twenty-four-hour access to course materials. CMSs provide a link to the Internet, the creation and automatic grading of quizzes and a grade book, and allow instructors to post course materials, a syllabus, and announcements. Readings can be posted via attachments or by scanning texts, and PowerPoint presentations, videos and podcasts may be added. CMSs also allow interactive communication from instructor to students and student-to-student via email, file exchange, discussion forums and virtual chat. A CMS may be customized by the instructor to suit teaching style and course content.

Before an institution chooses a CMS from the many on offer, there are the following major issues to consider:

- **Quality of product support**   The company should provide twenty-four-hour technical support and quickly resolve any problems that emerge with the system. Quality of support can be determined by contacting references or talking with technicians, administrators and instructors at other institutions.
- **Ease of use**   Navigation of the CMS should be relatively easy to learn, intuitive to the average user, and should not require a long period of training. Look at the various CMS websites for tutorials and demonstrations, ask for a representative of the company to come to campus to talk about their product, or seek a trial run of the CMS before you purchase. Contacting instructors at other institutions would also seem advisable.
- **Features**   The CMS should support all the features that instructors need in an online class, including newer tools such as podcasts, blogs and wikis.
- **Regular updates**   There should be a history of ongoing enhancement to the core product. Online technology and learning is constantly evolving, and the CMS should keep up to date with these changes.
- **Cost**   All educational institutions have to take into account the cost of the product. Nevertheless, cost should not be the first consideration when choosing a CMS. It is no use choosing the cheapest CMS if it is a poor product. It is best to pay a little more for quality.

The task of preparing an online class is made easier by many textbook publishers who now provide Internet-based software packages to help the busy instructor. These packages contain customized course material for teachers to use in conjunction with their textbooks. Some publishers simply provide online test banks, PowerPoint presentations and primary sources while others offer complete online course sites ready for use. The publisher-provided course site is available to an instructor as long as they assign the publishers' textbook to their students. If an instructor does decide to adopt a textbook site, they need to view these publisher-provided packages as teaching supplements, not as readymade courses. Publisher-provided materials do not necessarily cover the material that is most important to the instructor. Nonetheless, publishers' material can present the teacher who is new to online teaching with basic course content to which the instructor can add to during the course development process. Instructors should only use material from these cartridges that meet the goals of the course and ought to create their own assignments and assessments as needed.

Course management systems allow the teacher a large degree of control over the visual design of the course. It is vital to create a visually appealing, easy to follow, and welcoming course site. In some instances, institutions will demand a standard appearance and format for courses to facilitate ease of student use across multiple courses. Nevertheless, there are still ways to add graphic design to the course beyond what the standard format demands. It may be best to keep a simple, professional and serious tone to the course design, rather than overwhelm the site with visuals or technological gimmicks that confuse the students and make it appear that the instructor is not taking the course seriously. The title of the course and the course number, the name and perhaps a photo of the instructor, and some historical images in a pleasing banner or logo could grace the first page of the course (see Figure 1.1).

Instructors should focus on usability when designing the course site. Students should be able to find course material easily and intuitively. The course material can be made available in a number of folders that are plainly visible to the students and are appropriately labeled. It is possible to make a number of main folders and create subfolders as necessary. Folders may be devoted to announcements, discussion board, assessments, instructor information, syllabus and communication. A course documents folder could include subfolders for primary sources, websites, PowerPoint presentations, videos and audio selections. The instructor information folder could include a photo and a CV and provide a few sentences on the instructors' research interests, classes taught and some personal information (see Figure 1.2).

When designing a course, instructors need to be aware of copyright issues. Instructors cannot simply cut and paste portions from websites or scan whole articles or images into the CMS without permission from copyright holders. Neither can instructors post complete songs or videos in course sites; they are restricted to playing only a small portion of them. Making copyrighted material

Figure 1.1 Course home page

freely available to your students for dissemination is also prohibited. Instructors are allowed, however, to provide students with website addresses, to link to online databases for readings, and to use music, films or books found in the public domain. Instructors should always remember to give due credit to their sources. Colleges can also participate in the Open Course Ware (OCW) initiative introduced by the Massachusetts Institute of Technology in 2001 when they made some of their distance education curriculum material available for public use. The material is available at the *Open Courseware Consortium* website at www.ocwconsortium.org and can be freely copied for non-commercial purposes, but those who use it must give attribution to the originating institution and faculty. More than 50 colleges across the world now participate in the OCW initiative. As a precaution, always check with college administrators, lawyers or copyright offices about copyright issues when developing an online class.

Another issue to take into consideration when designing an online course is making arrangements for students with impaired hearing. Online courses should be accessible to all students—and they can be with a little forethought on behalf of the instructor. As a general rule, instructors must provide hearing-impaired students with accessibility to any spoken information. This means that narrated PowerPoint presentations should include text in conjunction with the visuals and sound. Movie clips need captioning, or a written transcript should be provided together with the video. Songs ought to have lyrics and maybe a

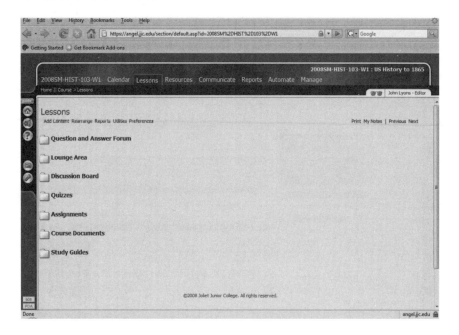

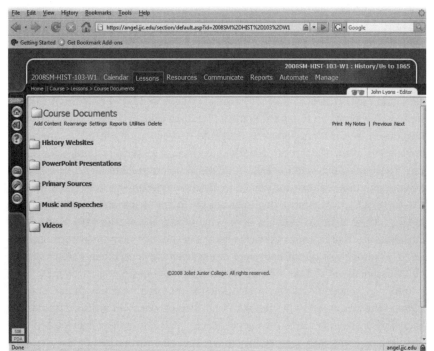

Figure 1.2 Course material layout

description of the song, posted alongside them. Most song lyrics can be easily found on the Web. Instructors need to include a written transcript of a podcast lecture or interview. This can be enormously time consuming to produce, but there is computer software such as Dragon NaturallySpeaking (www.nuance.com/naturallyspeaking) that can translate the user's voice into text.

Online courses can also be adapted for unsighted or partially sighted students. Windows accessibility options (found at Start–Programs–Accessories–Ease of Access) provides a magnifier that enlarges a portion of the screen and a narrator that presents audio of the screen content. Screen-reading software, such as JAWS for Windows at www.freedomscientific.com, creates audio for screen content and for the keyboard. ZoomText is a screen magnifier and text reading program that is available at www.aisquared.com. Speech recognition software, such as Dragon NaturallySpeaking at www.nuance.com/naturally speaking, can also be used by the visually impaired student to produce text.

The students

The content of the course changes depending on the type of student the instructor is teaching. Therefore, there are a number of questions concerning students that instructors need to think about when they design an online course. These include:

- Are students taking the course as a requirement or as an elective? This decision might affect the attitude and motivation of the students towards completion of the course material. Instructors can assign more complex material and undertake more peer evaluation if the students are highly motivated and interested in the subject.
- Are the students history majors? More class time needs to be spent on explaining to non-history majors why they need to study history and what benefits they will gain from a history education. Instructors can discuss with the students the relevance of the past in helping us to understand contemporary events, the benefits of critical thinking and analysis, and the improvements in writing, reading and speaking skills that studying history brings. The class may also need to spend more time on the basics (e.g. outlining the differences between primary and secondary sources and the mechanics of writing a history essay) if the students are non-history majors.
- What are the prior academic skills of the students? This affects the type and length of assigned research papers. Assigning a larger number of shorter papers, or requiring more than one draft of a paper, is preferable for students with fewer academic skills. Information on academic skills also helps the instructor assign the correct number and level of readings. If the

class is an upper level or graduate class, for example, there can be longer essays and more readings each week. You would expect an open-enrollment community college to have more students who need access to study guides on writing essays, taking notes, and reading sources than a graduate student from a four-year research university.

The instructor

Instructors need to receive adequate training before they attempt to teach an online class. They should be taught by the college's technical department in the use of CMSs and other online technologies. Instructors also need to learn the latest online pedagogy by reading journal articles and books before they attempt to teach online. It may be helpful to participate in an online course as a student in order to see the online experience from the students' perspective and to understand what makes a class effective. It is probably a good idea to have a mentor who can advise instructors in the development of an online class. At the same time, an instructor can talk to students and teachers about their online experiences and examine other online courses from a variety of disciplines.

When an instructor is adequately trained in online technology, they need to start designing the course. One of the first tasks is to think about course objectives, and what student outcomes the instructor wants to achieve in the course. What should the student be able to do upon completion of the course? What major historical questions will the course pose? The intended student outcomes and guiding questions will help instructors to choose the readings and assignments. Turning the course into a problem-solving venture with focused questions will also help to engage the students with the course content. Online learning can be just as passive as the traditional model unless the course assignments are built around probing questions.

To design an online course the instructor needs to know the differences between teaching face-to-face and teaching online. Online teaching lacks the body language that accompanies a traditional classroom environment. Students with bored or confused facial expressions, with their heads on the desk, talking to their classmates, or peering out of the window are indications for traditional classroom instructors that they are not engaging their students. In a face-to-face course teachers may then modify their teaching by clarifying the material or explaining the issues in a way that students can more easily understand. In an online class it is difficult to know if the instructor is engaging the students' attention or if students understand the material. Thus greater attention should be paid to eliciting student comments throughout the semester. In addition, the online instructor must pay more attention to motivating and engaging the isolated students to become independent self-motivated learners. This can be done by providing students with speedy, encouraging, and frequent feedback and by allowing students a large degree of control over what they do and learn in the course.

Because there is no close person-to-person contact between the students and the teacher in an online class, it is essential to personalize the online experience as much as possible and to establish a social environment conducive to learning. It is very difficult, but far from impossible, for an instructor to bring their personality to bear in teaching online and to build a rapport with the students; it just requires more thought and effort. Speaking in synchronous communication or in an audio or video recording makes it easier to convey a personality than the printed word can. Instructors should not be scared of communicating with their students by telephone. Some students like to hear the instructor's voice, and I'm amazed at how many of my online students insist on leaving a phone message in my office rather than sending me an email. The online environment also requires instructors to pay more attention to conveying a friendly demeanor in their written communication, such as in emails, discussion board contributions or assessment feedback.

Teachers also need to consider how much time they are willing to devote to teaching the class. The amount of time that instructors can spend facilitating an online class is endless. The first time you teach an online class is the most challenging. Creating a course site and transforming traditional pedagogy and activities into an online environment are enormously time consuming. Subsequently, however, instructors should have more time to add new activities to their course and correct mistakes they have made. With other classes to teach and a busy home life, instructors need to decide how much feedback students will receive, or how often they will contribute to the discussion board. Online teachers need to decide how often they will look at their email and whether they will be available to the students seven days a week or whether they will keep away from the computer on certain days.

Student support

Students new to online instruction will have to receive some help with the technology and academic work involved in an online class. Student retention is often a greater problem in online classes than in traditional face-to-face courses. Online students often feel socially isolated and many lack the self-direction and time management skills necessary to succeed online. Institutional support is crucial for student retention. Enrollment counselors could be used to interview applicants to see if they have the necessary skills for online learning. Colleges need to organize pre-course orientations, either online or face-to-face, to help students understand the technology used to deliver course content and provide

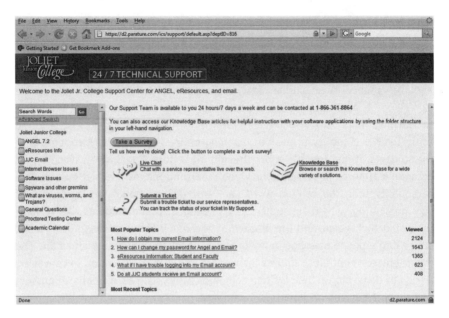

Figure 1.3 Technical support

information regarding course structure and policies. Once students are enrolled in the program, mentors may advise them on a one-to-one basis at regular intervals throughout the semester. In order to succeed online, students also need access to outside resources such as a writing center, an academic skills center, and a well-stocked library. Access to computers on campus with the appropriate software is also essential for students who may suffer technical problems with their own computers at home. It is also wise to ensure that a distance education website containing essential information is available and that students have access to technical help via online and telephone sources (see Figure 1.3).

It might also be beneficial to schedule a face-to-face meeting with the entire class at the beginning of the semester. This meeting may help teachers connect with the students, assist with team building and guide the students through the initial stages of the course. Some students who enroll in an online class, however, may resent having to visit the campus due to problems with transportation, work or family commitments.

Course organization

The course should be logically and simply structured in order to orientate the students and assist them in establishing a work routine. It may help the students if the course is built around a series of weekly assignments and assessments or it the course is divided into longer modules with each module including a series of activities and assessments and concluding with an exam. The appearance and content of each week's work, or module, should be consistent and made available to students in a predictable way. Avoid overloading the students with work at the start of the course when many are just getting acquainted with the technology and demands of online learning. It may be best to assign few readings and assignments during the first two to three weeks of the course and then increase the workload.

The instructor also needs to give serious thought to the deadlines for assignments. Some instructors allow students to set their own pace and open all their quizzes and exams to students at the beginning of the semester or apply flexible deadlines. On a practical level, however, it is difficult for students working alone to maintain self-discipline and motivation. Many students, both in traditional and online classes, procrastinate. If the deadline is the end of the semester, many students will start to do the work a couple of days before the deadline. As a result, students either do not complete the work or complete substandard assignments. Therefore it may be best to assign readings, quizzes and discussion board questions using weekly deadlines. These deadlines help keep students on track, and because students are working with the same class material at the same time, weekly deadlines assist in creating a greater sense of online community.

Syllabus

An online class requires a more detailed syllabus than a face-to-face class. Students need to know what to expect in the class and from the instructor. The syllabus should be seen as a form of contractual commitment between the students and the teacher in which the student has clear expectations about the course and understands the responsibilities they have undertaken in enrolling in the class. Careful consideration should be given to constructing a syllabus. It will often come back to haunt a teacher if important information is missing or misleading in the syllabus. Instructors should check with their history and distance education departments to make sure the syllabus is consistent with college policies. Indeed, it would be best to have a college-wide syllabus established that can be used as a model for all online instructors. The syllabus should contain clearly written and detailed directions and be broken into many sections (see Appendix A).

The syllabus for an online class should contain all the information that the student needs to succeed in the course. Instructors should include their name, location, and email address, but also their phone number and office hours so that a student can seek personal help when they need it. Include information on how to contact support services such as technical help, the Distance Education department and academic assistance. The syllabus should let students know how often you look at your email. It should contain the course name, course number, credit hours, prerequisites, and outline the technical requirements of the course. The course goals and course description should let the students know what they will do in the course and what the student learning objectives and outcomes are. The required readings for the course should be listed. A welcoming message and an outline of the commitments of the instructor and the students are also necessary. A section on academic dishonesty and netiquette will help to eliminate future problems. Policies on incomplete grades and withdrawal and drop dates should be included. The syllabus should list all course requirements and include due dates for all assignments, the consequences if the deadlines are not met and the weight of each assignment in the overall grade. Finally, the syllabus should include a weekly course schedule listing topics and all the weekly readings and assignments.

Announcements

The announcements page, the first thing the students see when they log on to the site, is an extremely important communication tool. During the first week of class, the instructor should post a welcoming message on the announcements page that lets the students know the instructor is available to answer their questions. The announcement may also remind the students to read the syllabus carefully and about the first assignments of the course. Throughout the semester, course announcements are essential means by which to remind students about due dates for assignments and for maintaining a regular link between the instructor and the students. Announcements can also be used to engage students with the material and personalize the class. Instructors can include announcements that mention new historical research, people or events that are in the news, and holiday greetings. Avoid using the announcements page for personal feedback or sensitive information, both of which should be reserved for email. The law in many countries protects the privacy of the students regarding educational performance and is a further reason to discourage individual feedback on the announcements page.

To add a little personality and fun to the announcements page, instructors can use SitePal, available at www.sitepal.com, which is an Internet-based subscription service that allows instructors to create animated speaking characters that can be added to the course site in place of, or in addition to, a written announcement. The instructor can choose to either record character messages using a microphone or to write the announcement and let the software turn the text into speech. The use of speaking animated characters engages the students more than a written announcement and personalizes the online experience.

Online teachers need to think deeply about designing and preparing an online class if they want students to have a productive educational experience. Learning theories should guide the construction of the course. By knowing the students and how they learn, online instructors can design a course that encourages learning. Instructors need to create a simple, easy to navigate course site and provide a detailed and clearly written syllabus. Once all this is done in a traditional classroom, teachers can then prepare lectures and provide expert instruction to the students. In an online setting, however, delivering a lecture is more complicated and is the subject of the next chapter.

Further reading

Bennett, Sue and Lori Lockyer (2004) "Becoming an Online Teacher: Adapting to a Changed Environment for Teaching and Learning in Higher Education," *Educational Media International* 41: 231–44. The two authors go into great detail about the way that online teaching changes the role of the instructor, increases the demands on them, and requires them to adopt new skills.

Bloom, Benjamin. S. (ed.) (1956) *Taxonomy of Educational Objectives: The Classification of Educational Goals: Handbook 1: Cognitive Domain,* New York: Longmans. The often quoted classic still offers sound advice on designing educational assignments.

Brookfield, Stephen D. (2006) *The Skillful Teacher: On Technique, Trust, and Responsiveness in the Classroom,* San Francisco CA: Jossey-Bass, second edition. A wonderful book that justifiably highlights the human side of teaching. This second edition includes a chapter on online education.

Chickering, Arthur W. and Zelda F. Gamson (March 1987) "Seven Principles for Good Practice in Undergraduate Education," *American Association for Higher Education Bulletin* 3–7. The seven principles provide a useful introduction to the idea that student engagement with the instructor, with other students, and with course material is the key to learning.

Chickering, Arthur W. and Stephen C. Ehrmann (October 1996) "Implementing the Seven Principles: Technology as Lever," *American Association for Higher Education Bulletin* 3–6. Update on the 1987 article, which discusses the role of technology in student-centered learning.

Duffy, Thomas M. and Jamie R. Kirkley (2004) *Learner-Centered Theory and Practice in Distance Education: Cases from Higher Education,* Mahwah NJ and London: Lawrence Erlbaum. A collection of essays in which contributors discuss the design of their distance learning programs.

Elbaum, Bonnie, Cynthia McIntyre and Alese Smith (2002) *Essential Elements: Prepare, Design, and Teach Your Online Course,* Madison WI: Atwood Publishing. An excellent book for preparing and designing an online course.

Gardner, Howard and Thomas Hatch (November 1989) "Multiple Intelligences Go To School: Educational Implications of the Theory of Multiple Intelligences," *Educational Researcher* 18: 4–10. This article helps us to understand the implications of Gardner's theory of multiple intelligences for education.

Graham, Charles, Kursat Cagiltay, Byung-Ro Lim, Joni Craner and Thomas M. Duffy (March/April 2001) "Seven Principles of Effective Teaching: A Practical Lens for Evaluating Online Course," *Technology Source*. A look at how the seven principles in Arthur Chickering and Zelda Gamson's "Seven Principles for Good Practice in Undergraduate Education" can be implemented in online classes.

Henry, Michael (November 2002) "Constructivism in the Community College Classroom," *The History Teacher*. Available from www.historycooperative.org/journals/ht/36.1/henry.html. Michael Henry suggests a number of practical uses of constructivist ideas in the history classroom.

Levy, Suzanne (Spring 2003) "Six Factors to Consider When Planning Online Distance Learning Programs in Higher Education," *Online Journal of Distance Learning Administration* 6. Levy surveys the literature on planning an online learning program in higher education and argues that a successful online course needs to pay great attention to student support and teacher training. The article also contains a good section on US copyright and intellectual property laws.

Ludwig-Hardman, S. and Dunlap, J. (April 2003) "Learner Support Services for Online Students: Scaffolding for Success," *The International Review of Research in Open and Distance Learning* 4. Accessed June 15, 2008 at: www.irrodl.org/index.php/irrodl/article/view/131/211. As Ludwig-Hardman and Dunlap make clear, institutional support is crucial for student retention. The authors provide some practical advice on how to provide this support.

Palloff, Rena M. and Keith Pratt (1999) *Building Learning Communities in Cyberspace: Effective Strategies for the Online Classroom,* San Francisco CA: Jossey-Bass. In a clear and detailed manner, Palloff and Pratt discuss how to design and facilitate an online class.

Wallace, Raven M. (2003) "Online Learning in Higher Education: A Review of Research on Interactions among Teachers and Students," *Education, Communication and Information*. A wide-ranging article that reviews research on online learning and is particularly useful for assessing the multiple roles of the online teacher.

Chapter 2

Reconfiguring
the lecture

COLLEGE TEACHERS TODAY MAY PUT more focus on student centered-learning in the form of cooperative learning and discussion than previous generations of instructors, but the time honored, and often effective, practice of lecturing remains a staple of the traditional history classroom. It is easy to see why. Lectures can be an efficient way to deliver information, to provoke discussion, and to explain concepts that are difficult for students to grasp. A passionate, well-organized, interactive lecture inspires students and engages them with the study of history. The excitement that is induced from interacting with a live audience, however, is impossible to reproduce online. Lecturing can still be used in an online classroom, but it is de-emphasized and students spend more time conducting their own research. Indeed, online teaching forces all instructors to be more inventive in delivering information and to come up with alternatives to the lecture. Many online teachers assign a readable textbook or post lecture notes, but more creative ways can be utilized to deliver a lecture online. Podcasts, videos or PowerPoint presentations can be employed in the online environment, or information can be imbedded in announcements or in course material.

Books

Textbooks, or selected history monographs, are excellent vehicles to deliver information to online students. Books can be viewed anywhere, which offers students more flexibility than they would have sitting in front of a computer to watch a video-taped lecture. Books are often easier to read than large amounts of text on a computer screen. Text for a computer screen can be reformatted to make it easier to read, but viewing a computer is often still less comfortable than reading a book. The structure and periodization of a textbook can also help the instructor—especially those teaching a course for the first time—to organize the course. Books may be used to form the basis of online discussions, or they may be used for background reading. To encourage students to read the books, instructors can assign quizzes on their contents.

There are, however, problems with using textbooks in an online class. New editions of textbooks are often published every two or three years, but publishers do not always update the supplementary material, such as the test banks. This can mean that course content no longer matches the new edition of the textbook and needs to be revised. To overcome this problem, several publishers are offering customized online textbooks, which do not have to be updated and can be used forever.

There are many types of history textbooks available for instructors to choose from. Choice depends on the academic interests of the instructor and the academic level of the students. To make it easier to read for online students studying on their own, the textbook in an online class needs to be well written with a strong narrative structure. It may also be best to adopt a concise or brief edition of a text rather than the comprehensive edition even though there is a tendency in some brief editions of texts to skim over major issues. Textbooks are often poorly designed visually and are often cluttered with minimally relevant illustrations. With so many visual images available on the Internet, it seems that a glossy highly visual text that contains large numbers of maps, artwork and graphics is not needed for an online class. Likewise, there is little need for a text that contains primary sources when so many are available online. The choice of textbook supplements is also a factor to consider. The inclusion of an instructor manual and a test bank could save teachers time and enhance the learning experience for the students. In the end, supplements are useful, but the quality and readability of the text are the most important factors to consider when choosing a textbook for an online class.

Posting lecture notes

One way to move a traditional classroom lecture to an online environment is to post lecture notes online. Lecture notes can replace the textbook or supplement it by going into greater detail on key issues. Either way, posted lectures should be mini-lectures that do not overwhelm the student with too much information. For students, written lectures are dry in comparison to a live lecture and hardly a suitable alternative. A less time-consuming and more visually appealing method is to provide links to information from websites. Then again, students can be directed to full-text online journal articles that are available through library databases. In both cases, however, the students are not able to hear an instructor's tone of voice, or see expressions or gestures, nor are they able to ask and receive immediate answers to questions concerning the lecture material. Instructors may therefore want to offer online students alternative ways of receiving information in the online environment.

Podcasting

Instead of posting the text of a lecture, instructors can post audio files online. A podcast, which is a contraction of the terms "iPod" and "broadcasting," is an audio file that can be downloaded from the Internet to a computer. Students can then listen to the podcast on the computer, transfer the broadcast to a portable digital audio player, or connect the audio player to a home entertainment center or a car radio. Students can listen to the lectures at any time and they can jump ahead if the material is too easy, or listen again if it is too difficult. Podcasting can be a great tool for instructors to record their own lectures or an interview with a guest speaker. By hearing the voice of the instructor, a podcast helps students establish a more personal connection to the instructor, and to the course. Most CMSs have recording capabilities for podcasts but there are other options as well. To create a podcast, you need a microphone and a software program to record the lecture and turn it into a digital recording. Audacity is one such program that records and edits sound—see http://audacity. sourceforge.net/. Textbook publishers are increasingly providing narrated podcasts, and videos, of the textbooks for the students.

There are some drawbacks to using podcasts to replace the classroom lecture. Podcasts do not always keep the online student's attention. Podcasts exclude important visuals, are not interactive, and lack the excitement of a dynamic classroom lecture. Some teachers may be self-conscious or uncomfortable recording their voice. Because of the average attention span, podcasts should probably be no more than fifteen minutes long. Listening to audio is slow to some listeners who prefer the speed of reading text rather than listening closely to a whole MP3 file. Many students listen to podcasts while doing other things such as driving, so they are unable to take notes. Therefore subject matter with a lot of detail should be avoided. Examples of ready-made history podcasts are provided in Box 2.1.

Video

It is, of course, possible to videotape a lecture. Instructors can create the video with a camcorder, digital camera or webcam and transfer it to the computer. The video can then be uploaded from the computer to a CMS, to the website *YouTube*, or another website that hosts video podcasts or vidcasts. There are some readymade videotaped lectures of leading historians available on the Web.

Box 2.1 Lesson plan: history podcasts

There are a number of readymade history podcasts available online that can be used in the online classroom. *Historical Podcasts* at http://historical podcasts.googlepages.com/ lists many of these. These podcasts are often a better option for instructors than recording their own lecture because they are often professionally produced and include interviews and discussions as well as lectures. A single episode of these podcasts could be used to replace a lecture. Here is a selection of history podcasts that I recommend:

- *BBC History Magazine* at www.bbchistorymagazine.com/podcast.asp: This is really an advert for the upcoming edition of the magazine. However, the podcast, which contains interviews with historians whose articles appear in the magazine, is informative and covers all areas of history.

- *Great Speeches in History* at www.learnoutloud.com/Catalog/History/ Speeches/Great-Speeches-in-History-Podcast/21306: Some of the speeches are original and some are narrated renditions. The quality of the speeches vary: a number of the narrations are rather dry while others are extremely moving. Selective use of this podcast could really enhance a history course.

- *History according to Bob* at www.summahistorica.com: Historian Bob Packett presents a series of short, and very entertaining, lectures that focuses on a wide array of topics.

- *History @ 33 1/3* at www.history3313.com/iWeb/History3313.com/ Home.html: This is presented by a professor of Middle Eastern History at Long Island University who interviews historians about their work. The interviews are very enlightening but tend to be a little too long. Still, a graduate class in history would find much of interest here.

- *In Our Time* at www.bbc.co.uk/radio4/history/inourtime: this is a radio program on the history of ideas presented by Melvyn Bragg and broadcast by the BBC. Each program is a roundtable discussion on a wide range of topics. Some of the programs focus on rather obscure topics but the discussions is always of the highest quality.

- *Talking History on Newstalk 106-108 fm* at www.newstalk.ie/ newstalk/podcasts.html: This is an excellent Irish radio broadcast. Like *In Our Time*, each episode is a roundtable discussion on historical topics but the topics are often more popular than those featured in the *In Our Time* broadcast but just as informative.

Princeton University, for example, has a large archive of lectures available at www.princeton.edu/WebMedia/lectures. In contrast to a podcast, instructors can use their body language to convey information on film and the ability to see the instructor creates a more direct connection between the instructor and the students. Another visual alternative is Tegrity Campus 2.0 available from www.tegrity.com, which allows the instructor to capture screen activity. With just a computer and a microphone, the instructor can record his or her own voice and demonstrate a concept or activity on the computer screen.

In spite of this, videoed lecturers often look stilted and videos lack the interactive nature of a real lecture. The attention span of students will probably be short when viewing video on a computer screen and it is best to show short clips. A video lecture also means that students are more tied to a screen to view the video and they do not have the flexibility of an audio broadcast. Because of this, video lectures should probably be used sparingly in an online course.

PowerPoint presentations

Presentation software that includes text and visuals are another powerful way to convey information. The most commonly used presentation software is Microsoft PowerPoint, but Apple has more recently introduced its own presentation software, called Keynote. The ease with which instructors can obtain cartoons, photos and paintings from the Internet, and the speed with which instructors can then have them incorporated into a presentation, makes presentation software very attractive. It is also possible to produce presentations with video and audio commentaries. Presentations are often best when instructors keep the number of slides to a minimum and the presentation relatively short with many visuals and little text. It is better to use high-quality photographs rather than clip art, which often looks gimmicky.

Articulate Presenter, available at www.articulate.com, is an excellent program if an instructor wants to make a lot of information available to students. Instructors can add audio narration to an Articulate presentation with the aid of a microphone. It reduces the size of the presentation so that it downloads faster and adds interactivity to a standard PowerPoint presentation. There is a list of slides in the Articulate navigation panel that makes it possible for students to move around the presentation. In addition, if students are unable to watch a presentation in one sitting, Articulate will ask them when they return to the computer whether they want to recommence the presentation where they left off (see Figure 2.1).

There are some problems with PowerPoint presentations, whether used in the traditional or the online class. Some images can be blurry and difficult to

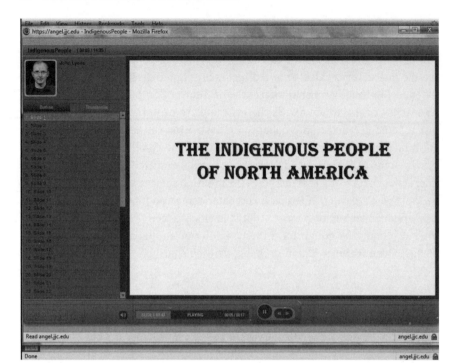

Figure 2.1 Articulate presentation

see. PowerPoint presentations with audio and text can often distract students. Too often students are furiously writing down the information on the slide and not listening to the presentation. PowerPoint presentations, like podcasts and video lectures, lack the dynamic character of a real interactive classroom lecture where the instructor responds to students' questions and comments. Like videotaped lectures, PowerPoint presentations have to be viewed on a computer and don't have the flexibility of podcasts.

Synchronous communication

Some instructors use synchronous technology to provide a live interactive lecture. Skype, for example, is a free program that offers audio and visual communication on the computer screen to those students who have a webcam, microphone and headphones or speakers. Skype also features instant messaging, file transfer and video conferencing. Some other programs combine synchronous with asynchronous communication and allow for audio, text, and visuals simultaneously. With Elluminate, for example, you can listen to a live presentation and view a whiteboard while communicating with the instructor and the other students. Elluminate allows the instructor to explain a concept while students see a visual representation and have the ability to ask questions through the microphone or through written text. It is beneficial to hear the voice of the instructor and hear or read the views of the other students. Elluminate personalizes interaction that is often depersonalized in text-based communication. Both Elluminate and Skype can be used for lectures or for the inclusion of guest speakers in the class. It is best to archive the presentations so that those who miss the live session can view it at a later date. Elluminate and Skype can also be useful for conducting office hours.

There are a number of issues that need to be considered before instructors incorporate tools such as Skype or Elluminate into online classes. As with a PowerPoint presentation, participants can be distracted from the Elluminate presentation because they have to read the text messages from other students or have to write their own contributions. The various buttons on Elluminate (leaving the room, hands up, smiley faces) also make the experience a little complicated. If students want to ask the presenter a question, of course, they have to listen live rather than to a recording from an archive. Students are attracted to online classes because they want a flexible schedule and resent being forced to be at the computer at a certain time. To schedule a time (or times if the instructor wants to offer multiple synchronous sessions) that is convenient for the teacher and all the students makes synchronous discussions difficult to organize. Finally, there are possible technical problems with these technologies. Students might need plug-ins and players to use Flash or audio, and students will need to know where to find them on the Internet. Students lead busy lives and make mistakes with technology when they are rushed, and many could be frustrated if they find they are unable to connect to the live lecture on time.

Announcements

It is possible to provide information to students without posting or recording a formal lecture. A weekly announcement is one way to do this. Announcements can be used to introduce a new topic or module. An announcement can put the weekly readings and discussions into context, summarize the major points of the previous week's work and clarify any misconceptions. These announcements can become, in effect, mini-lectures. Written communication such as this has another advantage compared to the more high-tech means of adding lectures. Podcasts, videos, PowerPoint presentations, Skype and Elluminate all require a high-speed Internet connection, but text in an announcement can be seen by those students who only operate on a dial-up connection.

Box 2.2 Quiz feedback

Here are five typical quiz questions I assign in my US history class together with the explanatory feedback to each of the five questions:

1 Which of the following Constitutional amendments abolished slavery?

   A 13
   B 14
   C 15
   D 16

The 13th, 14th and 15th amendments were all passed during Reconstruction. It was the 13th amendment that abolished slavery, the 14th amendment that allowed the federal government, not the states, to protect the rights of citizens, and the 15th amendment that granted the vote to African-American men. The 16th amendment had nothing to do with Reconstruction, but allowed the federal government to collect income tax.

2 Which region of the country was the most industrialized in 1865?

   A the North
   B the South
   C the West
   D all of it evenly

The US was very regionally distinct after the Civil War. The North was the most industrialized, and the South and the West were still agrarian.

3 In 1865 the Senate was chosen:

   A directly by the voters
   B by the state legislators
   C by the president
   D by the House of Representatives

Senators were chosen by state legislators until the 17th amendment was ratified in 1913. Initially, the House of Representatives was directly elected by the voters but the president was elected by an electoral college, chosen by the state legislators.

4 In 1865 the House of Representatives was chosen:

   A directly by the voters
   B by the state legislators
   C by the president
   D by the Senate

The House of Representatives has always been chosen directly by the voters.

5 The Civil War resulted in:

   A the death of more than 600,000 people
   B the political triumph of the North for generations
   C a growth in the power of the federal government
   D all of the above

The Civil War fundamentally changed the country. The war resulted in the deaths of more than 600,000 people, Northern domination of the country, and the diminished power of the states compared to the federal government.

Quiz feedback

The feedback section of online quizzes is another less obvious way to deliver information in the online environment. Instructors can embed a lot of "lecture" material in the feedback section of an online quiz. When a student accesses the answers to the quiz questions, he or she is confronted with explanatory information. The explanatory feedback should be the same regardless of whether a student answers correctly or incorrectly. Students can access the quiz questions, their answers, the correct answers, and feedback throughout the whole semester. This is a good resource when they study for exams or have to write papers. See Box 2.2 for examples.

Other ways to replicate the lecture

Information can also be conveyed throughout the course site. Instructors can add information to the study guides for an assignment. Written comments on returned essays can also be extensive and provide a focused way to transmit information. It is also possible to imbed lecture material in the discussion board when the teacher clarifies or expands on a student's contribution.

Classroom lectures are effective for providing basic information and often essential for explaining and giving context to assignments. Before students can analyze websites or discuss historical issues, they must have some basic background knowledge of the subject. There are a number of ways to provide basic information and reconfigure the lecture in the online environment. To reach the different learning styles of the students, it is probably best to include a number of the options mentioned here and to mix synchronous and asynchronous communication and audio, video, and text-based lectures. Nonetheless, online instructors need to rely less on the teacher's input via classroom lectures and more on engaging students in independent discovery and in student-to-student interaction. The next chapter considers one of the best ways to do both of these: the online discussion board.

Further reading

"Alternatives to the Online Lecture" (no date). Accessed June 15, 2008 at: www.ion.uillinois.edu/resources/tutorials/pedagogy/alternative.asp. A wonderful article that offers online instructors many alternatives to the lecture.

Brittain, Sarah, Pietrek Glowacki, Jared Van Ittersum and Lynn Johnson (2006) "Podcasting Lectures: Formative Evaluation Strategies Helped Identify a Solution to a Learning Dilemma," *Educause Quarterly* 29. Accessed June 15, 2008 at:

http://net.educause.edu/ir/library/pdf/EQM0634.pdf. In an informative article that has enormous consequences for those reconfiguring lectures online, Brittain *et al.* surveyed a group of first-year dental students at the University of Michigan and found that they preferred audio-only lectures over video and PowerPoint lectures because of the mobility associated with podcasting.

Deitz, Corey (no date) "How to Create Your Own Podcast—A Step-by-Step Tutorial." Accessed June 15, 2008 at: http://radio.about.com/od/podcastin1/a/aa030805a_2. htm. As it says, a step-by-step guide to making a podcast.

Finkelstein, Jonathan (2006) *Learning in Real Time: Synchronous Teaching and Learning Online,* San Francisco CA: Jossey-Bass. Everything you will ever want to know about using synchronous activities in the online classroom.

Fullmer-Umari, Marilyn (2000) "The Syllabus and Other Online Indispensables" in Ken W. White and Bob H. Weight (eds), *The Online Teaching Guide: A Handbook of Attitudes, Strategies, and Techniques for the Virtual Classroom,* Boston MA: Allyn & Bacon: 95–111. An excellent article that discusses the mechanics of producing a text-based online lecture.

Chapter 3

The discussion board

DOES THIS SOUND FAMILIAR? I walked into the classroom ready for a passionate discussion on the causes of the English Civil War. I had assigned my students two short articles offering opposing views on the origins of the conflict and had carefully prepared a series of discussion questions. I believed that the discussion would promote higher-level critical thinking skills by encouraging students to construct their own arguments and either defend them or refine them in the light of other counter-arguments. The discussion, however, flopped. Only five students contributed to the discussion; the rest were either intimidated into silence by the vocal few or proved unwilling or unable to articulate their thoughts on the subject.

The frustrating discussion described in my traditional classroom example compares unfavorably with the quality of asynchronous online discussions. Contributions to an asynchronous discussion are in written form and students are not online at the same time. Every student is required to contribute to an online discussion. Students who are shy and reluctant to speak in the classroom discussion are more likely to flourish in the anonymity of the online environment. By adding postings at a time convenient to them, online discussions allow students to have more time to reflect on what they have studied than they would have in a real-time discussion. Discussion questions directed at the wide array of historical sources available online can bring about a vigorous and thoughtful discussion. This, together with the ability to facilitate group work and provide social and informational forums, means that the discussion board is very popular with online students. Online discussion helps them to escape the isolation of the online environment and to establish a sense of community with other students in the class.

Design of the discussion board

The key elements in a successful online discussion are organization and forward planning. The instructor may create forums for as many separate discussion topics as he or she wishes. Many instructors create one discussion forum for each week and the questions concern different topics that chronologically follow the course sequence. Instructors can either assign one discussion question for the whole class or, to make the contributions less repetitive and the discussion more varied, provide each student with a different question or a choice of questions based on the same topic. After making an initial posting that directly answers the question, students are then expected to analyze each other's comments and respond to them in further contributions. To encourage students to write thoroughly and thoughtfully, it may be best to require a set length for the postings such as 250 words for the initial posting with each subsequent contribution a paragraph long. It is prudent to include in the syllabus a detailed outline of email etiquette, or "netiquette," which informs students how to make a meaningful contribution to an online discussion and which makes it clear that students need to be respectful to each other on the forums. A grading rubric and a sample post helps to establish clear expectations (see Figure 3.1).

It is wise to establish a strict deadline for discussion board submissions. One option is to post the discussion questions on Monday morning and allow

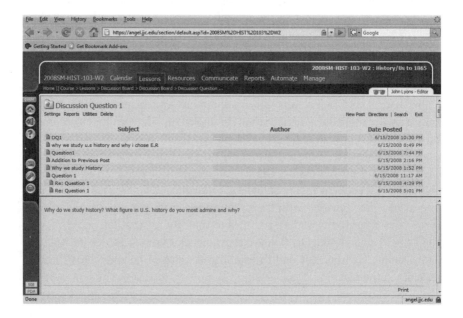

Figure 3.1 Discussion board

Note: Students' names have been shaded out of this figure to preserve anonymity.

students until Sunday evening to complete the assignment. The single Sunday night deadline, though, often means that students do all of the week's work at the last minute, which invariably leads to a less thoughtful discussion. An alternative is to require students to post an initial contribution by Thursday and the remaining postings by Sunday. By having a Thursday/Sunday deadline, students have more time to read other contributions and the quality of the discussion should improve. This can, however, annoy students who want to take advantage of the flexibility of an online class.

Discussion board questions

To elicit thoughtful discussion, the questions teachers assign to the discussion board need to be carefully designed. Questions that ask for yes or no responses, for correct answers or for the supplying of facts should be avoided. Instead, questions need to be open-ended and should encourage student interaction with one another and the higher-level thinking skills outlined in Bloom's *Taxonomy*. Scenario questions or ones that address controversial or provocative topics are ideal for provoking discussion. The first discussion questions I assign ask students why we study history and what figure in history they most admire. Neither question requires any substantial reading and both are designed to acquaint students with the idea of supporting their positions in writing. In general, it is often best to ask two interrelated discussion questions: the first lets students outline the argument of the source they have read or viewed and the follow-up question encourages students to think more deeply about the topic and if possible to bring outside knowledge into the discussion.

The discussion questions also need to contain precise directions to the resources the students need to answer the questions. The CMS is often over-loaded with course material, and there is nothing more frustrating for an online student than being unable to find resources because of unclear or imprecise directions. Instructors should let students know where to go to find the readings, videos or audios pertaining to the question, for example: "Go to the Course Documents folder, Primary Sources folder, The Indigenous People of the Americas folder, and read the article by John Heckewelder. Then go to the Discussion Board and answer the following question: According to John Heckewelder, what were the Indians' views of nature, religion, and property? How accurate do you think his views were?" Here, the students clearly know what article they need to answer the question and where they can find it.

The discussion board is an area where students can be introduced to some fantastic history websites. For ancient world history, for example, there are sites that provide students with insights into the lives of Egyptians, that bring the city of Athens to life, and that elucidate the ideas of Confucius. Students can go on virtual field trips to different museums and exhibitions or visit historical sites such as the Great Wall of China. Sometimes all the students could be asked to scrutinize the same website in great detail, and at other times they could be asked to look at a number of different websites and then share their insights with their peers. If students view the same website, the instructor may simply ask them: "What did you learn from viewing the website? What did you like most, and what did you like least, about the website?" It is best, however, not to be too dependent on one website because websites can sometimes disappear in the middle of the semester. Because of the variance in quality of material on the World Wide Web, those websites recommended by the instructor to the students need to have been previously evaluated by the teacher so that they meet established criteria for historically accurate content. Indeed, it may be best to take a little time to inform students how to recognize credible websites.

Instructors can also take advantage of the CMS's ability to display multimedia content by integrating music and speeches into the online discussion. Music and the spoken word are wonderful mediums through which to evoke feelings and emotions in students. Students can listen to musical selections and view the lyrics and then express their thoughts on the discussion board. For world history classes, it is possible to select music from the different cultures studied in the course. I post Native American music from the wonderful *American Roots Music* and *Song of America* compilations. I assign the old English folk song "Scarborough Fair" sung by Simon and Garfunkel and the old English drinking song "To Anacreon in Heaven," which later became the music to the "Star Spangled Banner," to demonstrate the influence of the British on the US. I also post drum and chant music from West Africa, and the African American spiritual "Go Down Moses" performed by Paul Robeson, to highlight the African influences on modern music. Students can listen to podcasts, and many websites, that include speeches and interviews with both prominent figures and ordinary people in history. For example, Prime Minister Winston Churchill's inspiring oratory, the passionate speeches of Malcolm X, and the memories of war veterans all come alive online.

The use of short video clips may also be helpful to illustrate key historical points and concepts and provoke discussion. For twentieth-century history classes there is a multitude of video clips available by linking to websites such as *YouTube*, *Google Video* and *Yahoo Video*. The speeches of key people in history, newsreel footage from the Second World War, overviews of historical events such as the fall of the Berlin Wall and images of protests from the 1960s can all be found online. It is probably best, though, to include only brief clips because the attention spans of students will probably be short when viewing video on a computer screen.

In addition to websites, audio files and videos, instructors may ask their students to examine and discuss a number of other primary sources online.

Box 3.1 Lesson plan: the market revolution

One simple visual can elicit enormous discussion online and enliven even the most unexciting of topics. For example, when teaching the so-called US market revolution of the early nineteenth century, I was looking for a discussion question that would hold the interest of my students by relating these economic changes to changes in people's lives. I displayed the following graph in the Course Documents part of the site showing the birth rate between 1800 and 1900. Women bore an average of more than eight children in 1800 but fewer than four children by 1900.

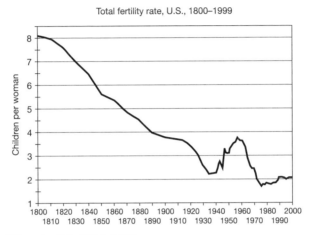

Total fertility rate, US, 1800–1999

Source: "Fertility, the Most Basic Questions." Accessed at: www.faculty.fairfield.edu/faculty/hodgson/Courses/so142/fertility/fertility.htm

After viewing the graph, I asked the class to go to the discussion board and to provide reasons for the decline in the birth rate. Once the class warmed to the subject, the braver suggested many reasons for the falling birth rate. With more men leaving the farm to go to work for long hours in factories, opined one, couples have less time and energy for sexual relations. Another suggested that people were too depressed to have sex!

Other, more serious, suggestions soon emerged. Single women going out to work had greater independence and married later. The separation of home and work provided women with greater power over the home and child rearing and they began to gain greater control over their own reproduction. Others suggested that the development of medicine and scientific methods of birth control and abortion reduced the number of babies born. This led to a brilliant discussion of the forms of contraception used in the nineteenth century. By the end of the lesson, students had a greater understanding of how a change in the economy leads to changes both in society and in the most intimate areas of people's lives.

By analyzing documents, images, and statistics, students are using the skills and tools of a historian (see Box 3.1 for an example of the usefulness of one simple graph). Because most people don't like to read too much on a computer screen, online readings, however, should be no more than one to two pages in length. Visuals such as cartoons (see Box 3.2), drawings, paintings (see Box 3.3), and photographs can be viewed singularly or joined together in a PowerPoint presentation.

Maps are essential to the study of history and particularly appropriate for online discussions. Many textbook publisher-created programs provide inter-active maps, or students could be directed to the thousands of maps available online. Large area maps can be used to help students visualize change over time, such as the rise and fall of empires, the migration of people or the urbanization of a particular country. Smaller, more detailed maps can illustrate battle tactics or the residential pattern of towns. Students could be shown a series of maps of the Inca Empire in the fifteenth and sixteenth centuries and asked to explain the expansion of the empire. A map of Europe before the First World War and another after the war could provoke discussion about German grievances that led up to the Second World War.

Simulations or role-playing games are often used in the face-to-face classroom but are even more suited to the online environment. Computer-mediated simulations are fun, and students learn without even thinking about it. Simulations require the student to play the role of a historical figure who is then faced with making a number of decisions in response to their assessment

---

Box 3.2 Lesson plan: using cartoons to view Britain in the nineteenth century

Cartoons are a fun way to engage the online learner. One such exercise involves students using *Punch,* a British magazine of humor that was first published in 1841. There are many website that contain Punch cartoons. For example, the *Punch* repository of cartoons at www.punch.co.uk, the website of artist John Leech Sketch at www.john-leech-archive.org.uk, and the *British Cartoon Archives* at http://library.kent.ac.uk/cartoons/collections/cartoonhublinks.php.

The cartoons could be used to examine British attitudes to gender, the Irish, Empire or British political figures or to specific events. Instructors could break the class into smaller groups with their own discussion board and send students to *Punch* websites to find their own cartoons, which they can then analyze and present to the group for discussion. Alternatively, the instructor could select one or two cartoons and ask the whole class to comment on them in the discussion board.

of the situation in which they have been placed. The Battle of Waterloo game online at the *BBC History* website at www.bbc.co.uk/history/interactive/games, for example, allows students to play the role of Napoleon Bonaparte or the Duke of Wellington. By participating in the simulation, students learn about the military tactics employed in the battle. In another online simulation, at

---

Box 3.3 Lesson plan: Westward Expansion

Discussions are often enlivened by incorporating art into the history curriculum. While discussing American views of Westward Expansion in the nineteenth century, one simple painting from the period can provoke enormous discussion.

I show the students the painting *American Progress* by John Gast.* The painting was completed in 1872 and is a fantastic depiction of the views of many in the new nation as it moved west. Gast, a white American painter, shares many of the same ideas as the journalist John O'Sullivan who coined the phrase "Manifest Destiny" to describe America's God-given right to move into Indian land. The painting shows a female figure in a white flowing garment at the center of the picture pointing from east to west with fleeing Indians and animals to her front and white Americans, trains and telegraph lines following behind her.

In place of a classroom lecture, students read a chapter of the textbook on Westward Expansion. This reading provides the students with the background information necessary to understand the different symbols and ideas behind the Gast painting.

The painting is presented in a three-slide PowerPoint display incorporating both audio and text. The first slide includes a few lines of text and a map of the US that explains the scale of westward movement from the end of the Civil War to the early twentieth century. The audio is a recording of the instructor reading the text. The second slide shows the painting *American Progress* by John Gast and includes text and audio that explains the background to the picture. The third slide presents the same painting, and the text and audio provide a series of questions that prompt the students to examine the painting in greater depth.

After viewing the PowerPoint presentation, the students must go to the discussion board and write a response to the following: "After viewing *American Progress* by John Gast, describe what you see and tell us what the main message or viewpoint of the painting is. What does the word 'Progress' mean here? Give specific examples." Students often find different facets of the painting to discuss, but all come away from the assignment with a greater understanding of how the US viewed Native Americans and Westward Expansion.

Available online at the Central Pacific Railroad Photographic History Museum at http://cprr.org/Museum/Ephemera/American_Progress.html.

www.schoolshistory.org.uk/westernfront/Western%20Front%20Sim.htm, the student plays the role of a British infantry officer on the Western Front in the First World War who is faced with a number of difficult combat situations. The student gains points by making effective decisions and loses points by making the wrong ones. On the discussion board, students might reflect upon the relationship between their own decisions in the simulations and the resulting consequences of their actions or discuss an element in the game that interested or surprised them.

Small group discussions

Because of the overwhelming number of discussion board postings in a large online class, it might be best to break the class up into smaller groups with each group having access to their own discussion board. Each group could then either follow the same procedure described earlier for a large class discussion or each week one student in the group could lead a discussion by summarizing the week's readings and providing a guiding question for the discussion. To allow students to generate discussion questions often induces deeper reflection and learning on the part of the student. Either way, a small group discussion often provokes a better and more varied discussion than one occurring in a large group.

Role of the teacher

The role of the instructor in facilitating an online discussion is just as important as his or her role in a face-to-face class. Rather than allow students to depend on the instructor for continual guidance and feedback, though, it is best to let the students take the lead. Instructors do not have to respond to every discussion thread. At the beginning of each week, simply set the context to the discussion question, and at the end of the week provide a summary feedback in an announcement. If a teacher makes a posting, students often respond to the teacher, and not to each other. The teacher then begins to dominate the discussion and suppresses the ideas and thoughts of the students. Just as in a traditional classroom, a good discussion ensues when the instructor does not intervene but lets the conversation develop on its own.

This "hands off" approach may not please all students. Many students are more comfortable with teacher direction and want to know the "correct" answer. Some resent the lack of teacher intervention. "No contact with the students, not involved in the discussions at all!" opined one of my dissatisfied students at the end of the semester. "Claimed he didn't want to influence the students thought process, isn't that what a teacher does? I felt the course was a real disappointment," the student concluded.[9] Others, however, seem to appreciate letting the students develop the discussion. Another of my students commented, "I love this man. He is sweet and so helpful and passionate about his subject. He reads every discussion board post, and analyzes them as a group, telling everyone what we did well on. It really gives you confidence in the class. The work is difficult and heavy, but if you work hard you will do well. He's great, take him!"[10] Thankfully, the latter view seems more prevalent!

Although too much teacher intervention should be avoided, a good online discussion still requires close monitoring of the students' posts, and some teacher input into the discussion may be necessary. Indeed, students like to feel that the teacher is reading their contributions and will intervene if necessary. It is definitely a good idea to enter a discussion if it is going wildly off-topic or if a student posts a serious factual error. Still, the instructor should provide students with a chance to refocus the discussion or correct the error before jumping into the conversation. To encourage discussion, not discourage it, instructor input into the discussion should be in the form of questions, not statements. Teachers should take action against inappropriate postings by deleting the offending posting and reminding the students about "netiquette."

Post-course evaluation

After the course has ended, the instructor should evaluate the use of the discussion board and make improvements: What topics, and questions, generated the most discussion? It is wise to remove, or at least rethink, those questions that generated the least discussion. Perhaps the questions need to be worded differently or more concisely. Did the students have enough information, or the right kind of information, to answer the questions? New editions of the textbook may require new discussion questions. Some websites may disappear and new ones need to be found or discussion questions refigured. It is also best to obtain student feedback from course evaluations to see if students preferred some questions over others or if they found the readings or other resources inadequate to answer the questions.

Informal non-graded discussion forums

In addition to the graded discussions, it is sometimes best to add non-graded discussion forums to the course. General question-and-answer forums can provide a place where issues and concerns connected to the course may be raised and addressed. Forums can deal with clarification of assignments, or with other

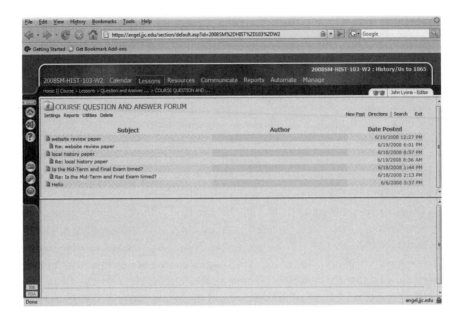

Figure 3.2 Question and answer forum

Note: Students' names have been shaded out of this figure to preserve anonymity.

issues that concern students. Students should be warned that the forums are not for private or confidential information, which should be reserved for emailing the instructor. Students post their questions and other students or the instructor provide answers. These forums save the instructor time answering individual emails on the same issues and students can access the forums at any time for the answers to their questions (see Figure 3.2).

Having a forum for off-topic social discussions is invaluable in an online class. Social forums help students get to know their fellow students and encourage a sense of community online. Students feel more connected to the course, which will help foster enjoyment of the course and increase retention. At the beginning of the course, the instructor could introduce themselves in an initial posting and then ask the students to introduce themselves. The introduction could include academic information but also some personal information. Student introductions online can be more detailed than in a face-to-face class, which has to contend with time constraints. An instructor could ask students about their hobbies, their favorite music, novels, films, or television programs. Or they could invite students to describe themselves in five adjectives or nouns, for example. Teachers could also ask students to post photos of themselves, something that younger students are quite comfortable with doing on social networking sites such as MySpace or Facebook. Student introductions can also be turned into a center of advice for learning online. Instructors can ask students what their biggest concerns or worries about studying online are. If they have studied online before, instructors could ask what advice they would give to help someone succeed online. Students can use this platform to voice their concerns and to obtain advice from their fellow students—advice that they will often heed more than advice that they receive during the course orientation or from the instructor. Students can subsequently post voluntarily. Sometimes students only respond to the social forums in the first week because they are not graded, but it is possible to encourage students to use them throughout the semester. Consider, for example, asking a new prompt question every few weeks. Tying the questions to events that are timely in nature may also increase student participation. Ask them about experiences they have had over the length of the semester. Instructors could also post their own responses. If students see that their teacher is engaged in the social forums, they may also be tempted to post.

It may be a good idea to employ a goodbye forum at the end of the course. An online course can often end abruptly. Students finish working on their final exams and projects and suddenly evaporate into cyberspace! Having a forum where both the instructor and the students can say their goodbyes provides a satisfying conclusion to the social component of the course. The forum can be used by students to comment on their experiences in the class, but the responses may be less than truthful if the grades have not yet been posted.

The online discussion can never replace the spontaneous and dynamic feel of a traditional classroom discussion, but a well-structured discussion board can often be far more rewarding for both teachers and students. One of my students, for example, suggested that the course "was good because you were able to make everyone interact with each other. I think I learned more from this class than a regular class setting because you were forced to voice your opinion. You don't have to share your views in the class room setting."[11] Another student commented, "I really liked the course. I liked doing the discussion board. Everyone contributes a lot of interesting perspectives. I think I have had better discussion in this course online than being at any of my on campus courses. They are all lecture and no real student discussions or opinions."[12] Not all student comments may be as positive but, in general, students prefer online to classroom discussions. Social interaction, improved higher level thinking skills, and bringing "history alive" can all be attained by using discussion forums. Because writing makes people think before they type, online discussions are often more thoughtful than classroom discussions and offer instructors the chance to encourage normally passive students to take a more active role in the class. Students engage in collaborative work with their peers and in the process learn to engage in rigorous debate in a respectful way. The use of academic and social discussion helps students break free from the social isolation often associated with online environments and promotes better student retention. As the next chapter shows, however, there are many other ways to engage students in online learning.

Further reading

Berge, Zane L. and Lin Muilenburg (2002) "Designing Discussion Questions for Online, Adult Learning" in Allison Rossett (ed.) *The ASTD E-Learning Handbook*, New York: McGraw-Hill: 183–9. The authors offer helpful advice on designing discussion questions for an online class.

Best of History Web Sites. Accessed June 15, 2008 at: www.besthistorysites.net/index.shtml. *Best of History Web Sites* contains reviews and recommendations of over 1,000 websites in all areas of history.

Kubricht, Paul (November 2000) "Reflections on Teaching International Cold War History Online," *Journal of the Association for History and Computing* 3. This is based on Kubricht's own experiences of teaching an online history class and offers some sound advice about designing an online class based around discussion.

MacKnight, Carol B. (2000) "Teaching Critical Thinking Through Online Discussions," *Educause Quarterly* 23: 38–41. This article provides some nuanced suggestions for using an online discussion board.

Martyn, Margie (2005) "Computer-Mediated Communication: A Quest for Quality" in L. Bash (ed.) *Best Practices in Adult Learning*, Bolton MA: Anker Publishing: 173–96. This article provides some astute guidance on how to facilitate an online discussion.

Palloff, Rena M. and Keith Pratt (2005) *Collaborating Online: Learning Together in Community,* San Francisco CA: Jossey-Bass. "In the online environment, collaboration can be seen as the cornerstone of the educational experience" (p. xi) insist Palloff and Pratt. The authors have provided a book that explains some basic concepts involved in collaborating online and that contains some practical activities that can be adapted to the history classroom.

Top History Games. Accessed June 15, 2008 at: www.activehistory.co.uk/top_activities/index.htm. This site provides a number of history simulations and games for school students that could be adapted to the college classroom.

Assessment

THE PROFESSOR IS AN EXPERT in European history. He has published widely, has taught the subject for twenty years, and has recently begun to teach online. Class assessments comprise a midterm essay exam, a final exam and an eight-page research paper. The exams, which include both essays and identification questions, are based on the course textbook. Essay questions examine the ideas of the Scientific Revolution, the causes of the French Revolution, and the role Stalin played in causing the Cold War. The research paper is a review of an assigned history book, *The Origins of the Second World War,* by A. J. P. Taylor, which was one of the professor's favorite books when he was in graduate school. The professor takes at least three weeks to grade the exams and the research paper. Comments on the exams and the research paper vary from "good work, well done" to "poor effort."

The story of this nameless professor, typical of too many college history lecturers who switch to the online environment, highlights the limited range of assessments that pervade many online history courses. Educational research recommends frequent and varied forms of assessments to accurately measure student progress toward the course goals and suggested student outcomes. A local history paper (see Box 4.1), an oral history project, a research assignment based around an analysis of a number of primary sources, journals, student projects, WebQuests, and a website review could engage students more effectively and make the study of history more exciting and relevant to them. Essays are certainly an excellent way to improve critical thinking, but other innovative forms of online assessment are now possible. Often included under the term "Web 2.0," web services and tools such as blogs, wikis and social bookmarks promote the sharing of information, interactivity and collaboration. In addition, the nameless professor should provide the students with a copy of his grading policy or a rubric to establish assessment criteria. His sparse, non-specific feedback was ineffective and did not help the students to improve. Whether in a traditional class or an online class, students need speedy, regular, and appropriate feedback on their assessments.

Box 4.1 Lesson plan: local history paper

One assignment that really excites students in my early United States history class is a local history paper. The local area played a role in the larger story of the US, and this paper allows students to find out about the role their area played in shaping, or being shaped by, history. Students start the paper by discussing the indigenous people who lived in the local area before the Europeans arrived. Then they examine the first European explorers and settlers and how they interacted with the indigenous people. By writing the paper, the students find out how the area was affected by major historical events such as the American Revolution, slavery, immigration, Westward Expansion and the Civil War. Students must use both Internet sites and books as sources for the paper. Books on local history can be put on reserve in the campus library, and local public libraries also have a collection of local history books. Students come away from the assignment feeling more connected to the nation's history.

Assessment in the online classroom

The online delivery of course content in Web-based courses necessitates different methods of assessment than those regularly used in traditional face-to-face classes. Assessment instructions have to be especially clear and explicit in an online course because there is a lack of verbal communication and non-verbal cues for the instructor to gauge students' understanding of the course material. What is normally done orally in the classroom, such as explaining the purpose and procedure of assignments, needs to be done in writing in an online class. Because of their lack of direct contact with instructors, online students require more feedback than a student in a face-to-face class.

Since Web-based technology offers a wide variety of assessment opportunities, instructors have many tools at their fingertips for creating new and improved forms of interactive and collaborative assessments. These different kinds of assessments are especially valuable as they often measure a variety of student abilities or Howard Gardner's intelligences. In this respect, having a variety of assignments can improve the authenticity of student assessment both in the online and face-to-face classroom. The following sections describe various online assessment options for the online history instructor.

Quizzes

Quizzes can be effective forms of online evaluation. CMSs allow various forms of quizzing: multiple choice, true or false, matching, fill in the blank, ordering and even crossword puzzles. Although many decry quizzes for their over-emphasis on rote memorization and promotion of lower-level, rather than higher-level, thinking, they do adequately measure comprehension and retention of the material. The use of timed quizzes may produce anxiety and affect performance in some students, but they do force online students to read the text rather than thumb through it for the correct answer. As an added bonus, students see the correct answers upon quiz completion, the quizzes are automatically graded by the computer, and the scores are immediately added to the student grade book. To assist the students with the quizzes, instructors could include practice quizzes on the course site and provide a study guide on quiz taking.

Quizzes can be turned into fun and interactive ways to assess students through the use of software programs such as StudyMate. StudyMate is a tool that creates a variety of review activities such as flashcards, pick a letter, matching, crossword puzzles and other games. Instructors may create these activities by hand, or they can import material from existing Microsoft Word files and other formats, or from publisher test banks.

Essays

Writing should be an extremely important component of any online history course. Essays elicit critical thinking and encourage creativity. The writing process is essential not only in clearly communicating one's ideas but also in developing and clarifying one's thoughts. Exams based on essay format are an excellent way to incorporate writing into the online class. Since online exams are typed and "open book," they are easier to read and usually of better quality than traditional "closed book" in-class exams. Instructors can also assign book reviews of non-fiction and historical novels or pose questions about the books. Biography and historical fiction help students understand how individuals experience large historical events. It is useful, and often more efficient, to grade essays using the Word insert and highlighting functions than doing so by hand.

Essays may be essential in the history classroom but assigning them can pose certain challenges as well. Crafting essay questions that will elicit the correct type of response from the students takes a significant amount of time and thought. The mechanics of grading online essays can sometimes be more time consuming than in a traditional class. For example, instructors have to download the essays from the course site, often in formats that then need converting to the instructors preferred format. Teachers then need to add comments to each essay, return them to the students, and assign a grade to the online grade book. If the instructor requires multiple drafts of a paper, or allocates a greater number of shorter essay assignments, even more time is consumed.

Blogs and journals

Blogging is another form of writing assignment popular in online education. Blogging comes from the term "web logging" and is used as a journal of reflection but also as a collaborative activity because blogs are open for debate and knowledge sharing with other students. Blogs can be available to the wider public on the Internet, or added to the course site to keep the discourse confined to the students enrolled in the course. Students can write on an instructor-assigned topic or on one of their own choosing. Students often spend extra time thinking and writing on blogs because their opinions are read by many others. Websites such as *WordPress* at http://wordpress.org and *Blogger* at www.blogger.com allow for the free creation and posting of blogs. *Edublogs*, at http://edublogs.org, is a free blogging service designed specifically for the educational community and suggests ways that teachers can use blogs in the classroom.

Another blogging idea could be for students to contribute to the online encyclopedia Wikipedia. Students could write a new entry or edit an existing Wikipedia article related to the particular subject of the class. Students could then post a brief summary of their entry onto the class discussion board, with a link to the appropriate page, and the other students could discuss the contribution.

Alternatively, students could write journals. They can be sent privately to the instructor via a course drop-off box or by email. Certain CMSs allow instructors to format a discussion forum as a private journal that only the student and teacher can see. Students can use these journals to reflect on what they have newly learned at the end of each week, and instructors can use the journals to assess student learning of the material.

WebQuests

A WebQuest is an inquiry-based assignment in which most of the information the students need to complete the lesson is found on the World Wide Web (see Box 4.2 for an example). WebQuests encourage critical thinking and are often built around cooperative learning. WebQuests, which were first developed by Bernie Dodge and Tom March at San Diego State University in the mid 1990s, have a standard format. They are organized into areas entitled "Introduction," "Task," "Process," "Evaluation" and "Conclusion." The "Introduction" explains the topic and purpose of the WebQuest. "Task" describes what the student should complete by the end of the project and is built around one guiding central question with a series of follow-up questions. "Process" clearly outlines the steps that the student needs to take to complete the WebQuest and lists the resources available to the students to accomplish the task.

Box 4.2 Lesson plan: WebQuests

One example of a WebQuest is the "Gilded Age WebQuest: Documenting Industrialization in America" (www.oswego.org/staff/tcaswell/wq/ gildedage/student.htm). This WebQuest examines the United States in the late nineteenth century. The term "Gilded Age" comes from a Mark Twain novel that described the corrupt nature of American politics during industrialization. In the WebQuest, students are required to produce a documentary about the period. Students are divided into groups, and each group is required to produce a segment of the documentary in PowerPoint using images and voice-over. Each group is required to design one of the following segments: technological innovation; big business; urbanization; immigration; and reaction to the period.

"Gilded Age WebQuest: Documenting Industrialization in America" is an exceptionally well-designed example of a WebQuest. The WebQuest is illustrated with some useful images that highlight the major issues. Navigation is seamless, the introduction is engaging, the task is well explained and doable, suitable resources are indicated, and a rubric is provided to guide the students. The WebQuest encourages cooperative learning and higher-level thinking skills. However, the Gilded Age WebQuest has its limitations. The WebQuest needs to have a longer introduction with a little more background information for the students. The guiding questions need to be more focused. There is no mention of historiography and the opposing views of historians on the period.

"Evaluation" lists measurable ways to assess the student's work, most often with the use of rubrics. "Conclusion" reminds students about the most important points they have learned. There are thousands of readymade WebQuests available on the Web. Tom March hosts a website that lists what he considers to be the best WebQuests (http://bestwebquests.com/about/default.asp).

WebQuests have now become the buzzword at teaching conferences and workshops, but they have their limits. They take an enormous amount of time to produce. The research questions have to be carefully chosen, websites found, and the WebQuest constructed. Finding websites to use in a WebQuest is very time consuming. Many history websites are ill-informed and poorly produced. Although many WebQuests are available on the web, most of them are produced for elementary or high school—not college—students, and many are badly designed. Indeed, some are not WebQuests at all, focusing on recall of knowledge rather than critical thinking. Some of the websites and WebQuest links can disappear into cyberspace during the semester, leaving the instructor and the students extremely frustrated. In many ways, WebQuests are too focused. Students do not have to design research questions or find useful websites for themselves. Instead the instructor guides the student and does not allow the student to fully research his or her own topic.

WebQuests are certainly valuable for incorporating technology into learning and increasing higher-level thinking skills. They are ideal for open-ended questions, which are the main focus of history courses. To help instructors construct a WebQuest, or to assist in deciding which readymade WebQuest to use in the course, Bernie Dodge and Tom March at San Diego State University have developed a resource to guide teachers (*WebQuest.org* at http://webquest. org/index.php)

Website reviews

A website review is an important form of assessment because so many students use websites in research papers, and because websites are a major component of an online class. By analyzing a website, students study a historical topic in depth and come to appreciate the need to critically examine the sources they are using. The students could examine the same website, one website from a pre-approved list, or choose their own to review. A website review could analyze one website in great detail or compare two websites. One site maybe less biased than the other, one maybe better designed, one may have more information and resources included in it, or one maybe more historically accurate (see Appendix B).

E-portfolios

Students can also be assessed in an electronic portfolio, also known as an e-portfolio. E-portfolios are a collection of digital work, such as sound, images, and text, which are gathered over the length of the course and can then be displayed online. The students have to organize their portfolio around a topic or theme of the course. They display creativity in choosing the topic and the artifacts. Students have to provide a justification for the inclusion of the artifacts and reflect on what they have learned throughout the course. The e-portfolios can be assessed by peers, revised by the student and then graded by the instructor. In this respect, e-portfolios allow students to truly self-direct their own learning, and to showcase their intellectual development.

Video, podcast and PowerPoint presentations

The relatively easy access to technology, and the desire of students to use it, means that students can produce and post their own video, podcast or PowerPoint presentation. The presentation could be in the form of a first-person or third-person report. "My life as a soldier" or "Stalin's thoughts on the postwar world," for example, would prompt students to exhibit thinking in a highly creative way. Students could incorporate text, visuals and audio into a PowerPoint presentation and post them into the CMS for the rest of the class to view and comment on. Because some students may not have access to the technology, these projects could be offered as an alternative to an essay assignment or used as an extra credit assignment.

Social bookmarking

A short, but useful, assignment is made possible with social bookmarks. Social bookmarking allows students to access "favorite" Web links from any computer anywhere in the world. These favorites can then be shared with others. Students can be assigned to find resources on various topics, which they can then share with other students. These resources can also be used to benefit the instructor in research or teaching. One example of a social bookmarking application is del.icio.us (http://delicious.com).

Getting away from the computer

Just because their course is taught online, instructors should not refrain from taking advantage of offline resources in the local area that can enrich the learning experience (see Box 4.3). Students can be assigned to see a movie in the local cinema or rent a video from the local store. They could visit an exhibition, a historical archive, a place of worship, a lecture, a local historical museum, or a historical site. These trips could be optional extra credit assignments or a mandatory part of the course. If they are mandatory, it is wise to highlight these extra activities in the syllabus so that students know what to expect at the beginning of the course. It is probably better that the students visit in their own time rather than as part of a class field trip, which would be difficult to organize because of conflicting schedules. They could be required, for example, to visit during a specific time frame and to sign a sign-in sheet that the instructor can pick up at the end of the assignment. Students could then write a reflective essay or blog about their experiences.

Box 4.3 Lesson plan: oral history project

Students enrolled in my "World History Since 1500" courses take part in an oral history project. As part of the project, students conduct a tape-recorded interview with their oldest living relative and with the information they obtain they write an eight-page essay that seeks to show how their family shaped, and was shaped by, history. The taped interviews are then archived at the local Historical Museum. I provide the students with two copies of a "Consent for Participation in Research" release form, which is required to allow the instructor to post the audio tapes online or for researchers to use the tapes at a later date (see Appendix C). I then deposit the tapes, the essay, the consent form, and a photo of the interviewee in the museum archives where they can be used by historians studying the local area. The information unearthed in the student interviews provides a wonderful window into the lives of the diverse group of people who live in the local area. While conducting the interviews, students have shown a greater interest in the study of history and links have been forged between the college and the students' families, the local historical society and historians in the community.

Small group work

Cooperative learning through small group work, increasingly essential in the traditional face-to-face classroom, can also be adapted to an online class (see Box 4.4). Collaborative learning means that knowledge can be shared among the group. Students learn how to work together, and the process often engages the learners who enjoy problem-based learning. Group work also encourages student-to-student interaction and breaks down the isolation associated with online learning. Groups could design PowerPoint presentations on important figures in history, review a website or analyze a historical film. Each group could have access to a discussion board to facilitate communication. Group projects work best when instructors provide students with a timeline for each stage of the project. A grade could be assigned both to the group as a whole and to each individual group member.

Wikis, which are web pages that can be created and edited by invited users, are perfect for online group projects. Instructors and students can post content online without the need to master Web-building skills. A teacher can see exactly which students have contributed or edited the content of the wiki. Instructors may set up a wiki at *Wikispaces* (www.wikispaces.com) or at *Google Docs*. A lot of wiki hosts have commercial advertisements and pop-ups that are distracting. An alternative site that is geared towards academic student wikis is www.wikieducator.org.

Small group work in an online class involves as much, if not more, organization on the part of the instructor as group work in a traditional face-to-face classroom, but it is often more convenient for students. Online group projects have to be even more organized in terms of instructions and logistics than in face-to-face classes. At least in a face-to-face class there is more opportunity for the instructor to iron out problems, since the groups meet regularly during class time. Conversely, students often find it difficult to accomplish group projects in traditional classrooms, especially on commuter campuses, because students have different schedules, which make it tricky to arrange group meetings outside class hours. Online technology, however, facilitates group work by allowing file sharing and communication at distance and at different times.

Online group activities, just like group projects in the face-to-face classroom, may be problematic. Some students are highly motivated while others want to do little of the work, which can cause enormous frustrations and conflict within the groups. Many online students prefer to work alone, at their own pace or at a time of their own choosing and do not want their grade to depend on

---

Box 4.4 Lesson plan: small group debates

Many types of small group debates are possible online. The instructor could break the class up into teams with each team taking opposing sides on major historical issues. A private discussion board could be provided to each group, along with a common discussion area where the inter-group debate takes place. Each group could provide an opening statement. After reading the statements, the groups could ask questions about the other group's position, provide rebuttals, and add closing statements that could all be posted by a specified date. Members of the groups could take different roles: the organizer, the researcher who finds the sources, the editor and poster of the initial posting, the summarizer, the person who composes questions to ask of other groups, and the person who rebuts the questions.

Groups could also engage in role playing. In fact, role playing often works better in an online class than in a face-to-face one, because students tend to be less nervous in the anonymity of the online environment.

CMSs also provide the option of "fishbowl" debates, in which two participants or groups debates an issue while the rest of the class acts as the audience. The rest of the class could then use the discussion board to discuss the merits of each case.

the work of others. A poorly designed group project often leaves students contributing sections of the project as individuals rather than truly collaborating with others. Some of these pitfalls can be avoided by providing clear directions and impressing on the students the benefits of online group projects. The instructor can switch students from one group to another if they fall out with members of their original group. Finally, the instructor can assign a group grade and an individual grade, with the latter comprising the bulk of the grade. By using an online discussion board and a wiki, the instructor can track the individual contribution of each member of the group and make it easier to apply individual grades (see Appendix D).

Rubrics

One way to help students with their assignments is through the use of rubrics. Rubrics outline the criteria that student performance will be graded on. Rubrics can be holistic, i.e. score the overall assignment, or analytic, i.e. score individual parts of the assignment such as introduction, conclusion and sources. In an online class where clearly written instructions are even more important than in a face-to-face class, rubrics can be extremely helpful to students. They make clear to students the relative importance of each component of an assignment. Rubrics provide students with the instructor's expectations and help students formulate a work plan when starting on a new assignment. Rubrics are also useful for instructors as they make teachers think about how they grade and make them pinpoint the components of a good essay or other assignment. By clearly highlighting a good paper from a bad one, instructors can expect better student performance. Rubrics should be included along with the instructions for each assignment and maybe some practical examples so that students can get an idea of what constitutes quality work. Sample rubrics are available at *Rubistar* (http://rubistar.4teachers.org/index.php), which is a free online tool to help instructors create rubrics (see Appendix E).

Evaluation and feedback

Instructor feedback is essential to helping students improve their performance. In addition to a numerical grade, students need written feedback that provides them with information about how well they performed. Comprehensive, encouraging and frequent feedback is necessary in any class, but is particularly important in the online environment where contact between students and the instructor is limited. In particular, feedback should contain information about what was, and was not, accomplished. Instructors could provide practical examples to guide students in the future. Teachers should grade each student's work in a timely manner, so that the student can learn from the instructor's feedback prior to working on the next assignment. Instructors should tell the students when they can expect their graded assignments returned.

There are a number of ways to provide feedback online. Teachers can send each student an email message assessing the performance and providing a grade. A more personal touch is to send each student a recorded audio message. Alternatively, the instructor can provide feedback to the whole class in an announcement. A synchronous tool such as Skype can be used very effectively to provide feedback to students. The instructor could arrange a general time for all the students to check in and ask questions, giving them an opportunity to gain feedback from both the instructor and classmates. Otherwise, the instructor could set up individual meeting times on Skype to provide specific feedback to individual students, especially when privacy is needed to issue grades or criticism.

Peer assessment

Most of the educational research suggests that peer assessment enhances student learning and should be part of the learner-centered classroom. Peer review can help students break out of the isolation of the online environment and promote collaboration among students. In theory, students will receive more feedback than over-worked instructors can provide, they will gather ideas from multiple sources rather than from the single teacher, they will produce better-quality work due to peer-pressure motivations, and they will enjoy a greater sense of online community. In effect, students can now grade each other and allow the instructor to undertake other work.

Before teachers start to celebrate and assign multiple peer assessment assignments, they need to be aware of the pitfalls of peer review. On the one hand, many students have little passion or interest in the subject of the course, never mind the content of other student papers. On the other hand, eager students might have the motivation to be overly critical of other students' work in the hope of impressing the teacher. Rather than help to build online cohesion and collaboration, peer review can have the opposite effect and create antagonism between students and between the students and the teacher. Students often are hostile toward peer assessment in their courses because they want expert instruction from the teachers and believe they are in class to be taught not to teach. To avoid these problems, instructors need to take time to prepare the peer review assignment. Impress on the students the benefits of peer review and avoid making the assignment a major part of the grade. Students need to be carefully told what to look for when assessing other people's work. Providing them with a rubric is certainly a good idea (see Appendix F).

Classroom assessment techniques

Another way to assess student learning, and faculty effectiveness as teachers, is to use a classroom assessment technique (CAT). Without the cues and personal interaction found in a traditional class, it is difficult to know if the instructor is engaging the students' attention or if students understand the material in an online class. Therefore instructors should assign short non-graded assignments to monitor student progress throughout the semester. One example of a CAT is a "Minute Paper." At the end of each week, for example, students could briefly answer the following two questions in less than 100 words: "What was the most important thing you learned in class this week?" and "What important question remains unanswered in class today?" Another example of a CAT is a "Muddiest Point." Students are asked to briefly answer the following question: "What was the muddiest point in the class this week?" Alternatively, instructors could periodically ask the students what they like or dislike about this week's class or the class so far. The students could answer these questions in a short contribution to the discussion board or by sending an email to the instructor. Instructors can provide feedback for CATs in weekly announcements. The announcement could clarify the muddiest points and provide more information to students to address the problems outlined in the minute papers. Depending on the problems outlined in the CATs, instructors could make adjustments to the course content.

Two problems exist with CATs in an online course. Students in a traditional class can take CATs anonymously at the end of the class and leave them on the front desk for the instructor to pick up. An online teacher needs to give more thought to maintaining the students' anonymity. To remain anonymous, the instructor would need access to an online survey tool to administer the CATs. *SurveyMonkey.com* is a website that can be used to create anonymous online surveys for students. However, if the CATs are not graded, the students may not put any effort into completing them. It may therefore be best to assign CAT as extra credit assignments, with students receiving points for completing them on time.

Student evaluations

Student evaluations of the course can be beneficial to both students and instructors. Evaluations undertaken either during the course or at the end of the course could ask students to provide their views on course content and assignments. Students need an area to complain and vent their frustrations. In a classroom they can do this with their classmates but in an online class they are alone. The evaluations let the instructor see the course from the students' perspective and let them know if they are engaging the students' interest in course material. The student evaluations can help the instructor make revisions to the course for the following semester.

Many instructors wonder how effective student evaluations are. In online classes, only a few students bother to complete the evaluation forms and many put very little thought or effort into them. Once instructors have taught a class for a number of years, the comments look the same semester after semester. Nevertheless, there is much value to student evaluations, and it is better to gain some feedback from students than none at all. Instructors can vary the questions if the responses are repetitive and tailor the questions toward specific class assignments or readings. Thoughtfully designed questions will increase the number and quality of responses. On some questions, provide students with an option to write in their own answers or to explain their answer. Student surveys should be anonymous. They should also be short; no one wants to fill out a long survey. If a survey is too long, the quality of the answers usually start to taper off towards the end (see Appendix G).

Student evaluations are necessary but of limited value because instructors also need to know the opinions of students who dropped an online class. Student evaluations only focus on those who successfully completed the course. It is a good idea to survey students who withdrew from an online class to find out their reasons for dropping. College administrators could supply students who drop an online course with a voluntary and anonymous survey to find out why they failed to complete the class.

Continuous assessment should be a major component of teaching online. Many forms of assessment are possible in an online history class. Quizzes are an efficient way to encourage students to read the course textbook and to memorize information. However, for a history course, writing assignments should comprise a significant portion of the students' grade. Evaluating a student's writing provides the instructor with the best insight into his/her critical thinking skills. In addition to written exams or essay papers based on assigned books, assessment in online history courses could include website reviews, WebQuests, discussion boards, blogs and journals. Students who undertake an online class need to be exposed to a variety of historical sources and projects both online and in the local area. Local areas have resources such as libraries, museums, and people with stories to tell, which can be integrated into the online experience. As much as possible, instructors should also let students choose their own assessments or assignment topics. Students will engage with the material more, and produce better work, if they have an interest in the topic. In addition, students need appropriate feedback from a variety of sources including the instructor and other students in the class. Rubrics help students to understand the important points of an assignment, while student evaluations and CATs can assist the teacher in deciding if the assessments are useful.

Further reading

Angelo, Thomas A. and K. Patricia Cross (1993) *Classroom Assessment Techniques: A Handbook for Faculty,* San Francisco CA: Jossey-Bass, second edition. This is the classic text on classroom assessment techniques and contains many suggestions for gathering feedback on teaching and student learning.

Conrad, Rita-Marie and J. Ana Donaldson, (2004) *Engaging the Online Learner: Activities and Resources for Creative Instruction,* San Francisco CA: Jossey-Bass. This book describes many activities that can be used in the online classroom; most are not connected with the study of history but can be adapted to the online history class.

Dawley, Lisa (2007) *The Tools for Successful Online Teaching*, Hershey PA: Information Science Publishing. Lisa Dawley does an excellent job in describing the strengths and weaknesses of online tools commonly found in a CMS, and she offers some useful ideas for assignments.

Grant, Lyndsay (2006) "Using Wikis in Schools: a Case Study," *Futurelab Online*. Accessed June 15, 2008 at: www.futurelab.org.uk/resources/documents/discussion_papers/Wikis_in_Schools.pdf. This article examines the use of wikis in collaborative learning. In a case study that involved the use of wikis in a UK secondary school, Grant clearly suggests that many students wanted to contribute as individuals in group projects and were often frustrated by their collaborators.

Kerka, Sandra and Michael E. Wonacott (2000) "Online Assessment: Principles and Practices," *Practitioner File*. Accessed December 5, 2007 at: www.cete.org/acve/docs/pfile03.htm. Discusses the principles, techniques, and challenges of online assessment.

Lorenzo, George and John Ittelson (2005) "An Overview of E-Portfolios." Accessed June 15, 2008 at: http://net.educause.edu/ir/library/pdf/ELI3001.pdf. This paper provides an excellent introduction to e-portfolios and includes some examples.

Trinkle, Dennis A. and Scott A. Merriman (eds) (2001) *History.edu: Essays on Teaching with Technology,* New York: M. E. Sharpe. The authors in this collection examine the many uses of the World Wide Web in teaching and researching history. The book says little about online classes specifically but contains some good ideas about teaching with the Internet.

Watkins, Ryan, *75 e-Learning Activities: Making Online Learning Interactive* (2005) San Francisco CA: Pfeiffer. This book describes some excellent activities that can be incorporated into the online environment.

Williams, Jeremy B. and Joanne Jacobs (2004) "Exploring the Use of Blogs as Learning Spaces in the Higher Education Sector," *Australasian Journal of Educational*

Technology 20: 232–47. Drawing on data from students in an MBA program at the Brisbane Graduate School of Business, Williams and Jacobs found that blogs provided an effective tool for teaching and learning. The authors suggest that blogs can engage students in collaborative activity, knowledge sharing, reflection and debate.

Zariski, A. (February 1996) "Student Peer Assessment in Tertiary Education: Promise, Perils and Practice" in J. Abbott and L. Willcoxson (eds) *Teaching and Learning Within and Across Disciplines*, proceedings of the 5th Annual Teaching Learning Forum, Murdoch University, Perth: Murdoch University: 189–200. In a well-balanced essay, Archie Zariski helps us understand the drawbacks to peer assessment. The author suggests that significant guidance is needed to incorporate peer assessment into teaching practices.

Chapter 5

Classroom management

I N FACE-TO-FACE CLASSES, instructors have to impose rules and regulations to ensure that the behavior of students is conducive to learning. Attendance, tardiness, talking in class and plagiarism are all issues teachers have to deal with in the traditional classroom. In an online class, instructors have to address some of these problems and many others. Plagiarism is probably more prevalent in an online class because assignments are completed in the privacy of the student's home and there is so much information available to students to download from the World Wide Web. Other issues such as improper email communication and technological problems play a large role in the online environment. Classroom management in an online class is not just a question of controlling student behavior, however; it also a matter of understanding and alleviating student stress.

Cheating and plagiarism

The anonymity of an online class can lead to problems with academic dishonesty. Because students are unsupervised, instructors can never be sure whether it is somebody else doing the work of an online student. New technologies have made it easier to cheat. Websites providing free term papers to students have proliferated. Students, away from the prying eyes of the instructor, are tempted by cutting and pasting from the vast array of websites that are available at their fingertips.

Many of these problems of academic cheating can be avoided. Some instructors insist on students coming to campus to take proctored exams as the only way to verify that the students registered for the class are really doing the work. However, some online students may find it difficult to travel to campus for a proctored exam. Many have child care issues, some may be physically challenged, and others may be working or living out of state or out of the country.

Many of the students who enroll in an online class expect to do all the work online and not to have to come to campus.

Instructors can employ a variety of other methods besides proctored exams to prohibit academic dishonesty. Students will more likely want to learn the material, not cheat, if the assignment is relevant, fun and engaging. If instructors establish a personal relationship with the students, a student may not want to let a teacher down by cheating. Instructors should insert a plagiarism warning in the syllabus because many students may not know that plagiarism is a major form of academic dishonesty. Some CMSs permit the instructor to block student views of the discussion board so that students have to post their contribution first before they can see the postings of other students. The ability to time quizzes and randomize questions from a question pool means that no student has the same set of quiz questions, which makes it more difficult to dishonestly acquire the answers from another student.

Plagiarism in essay exams can be prevented by assigning topics and assignments that are unusual. Instructors need to be creative with essay questions and thereby avoid assignments that are often easily available on student essay websites or downloaded from the Web. For example, ask the students to imagine they are a historical figure and have them explain how they would experience a particular historical event. Teachers could assign research papers on local history or an oral history project. They could ask students to write about specific passages from an assigned book or about a particular list of primary sources. It is probably best to avoid assigning over-used books for assignments because they provide many possibilities for plagiarism on the Internet. Changing essay questions each semester should prohibit students from using the papers of those who previously took the class.

In addition to avoiding plagiarism, instructors need to be able to detect it when it occurs. Instructors can keep old papers on file for comparison with students who previously enrolled in the class. Search engines can be utilized to find plagiarism. Another way to detect plagiarism is to tell students to turn their work into a plagiarism detector website such as *Turnitin.com*. *Turnitin.com* is an online database that compares a submitted paper to student papers previously submitted to *Turnitin.com*, to information on the Internet, and to databases of journal articles. Letting students know that these methods are being used to detect plagiarism may deter plagiarism before it happens. If plagiarism is detected, the policy of the college or the department should be followed. A "fail" for the work is often considered to be the minimum action to be taken, to discourage further cheating. If cheating occurs more than once, dropping students from the class and notifying the college would seem appropriate.

Emails

A further problem in online classes concerns the frustrations with communicating in written emails. Emailing makes instructors more approachable and accessible to students. One of the outcomes of this, and a problem that online teachers complain about most, is that students can be too informal, demanding and inappropriate in their correspondence with the teacher. Students who would be careful to approach or criticize teachers in the traditional classroom prove much less reticent with the impersonality of an email. Online students are much more likely to question grades, to ask teachers for extended deadlines or to cajole the instructor into assigning more lenient and undeserved course grades when they write in the isolation of their home than when they have the teacher in front of them. Tone of voice can help to convey an intended message accurately but this is not the case with online communication where the written word is blunter. Emails can appear to imply things that the author never intended or the content may be acceptable to say in person but can seem harsh in tone on paper.

There are many ways to overcome these problems. To help establish a good relationship with the students, it is wise to address the email to a student by name and sign your own name at the bottom. An instructor's written communication should be polite, friendly and supportive. It is best to try to avoid blunt, assertive language. Emails can often be misinterpreted, and adding humor to written communication just adds to the problem. Adding sarcasm or irony to an email can be funny to the sender but offensive to the recipient. It is best for teachers to carefully proofread emails before they are sent. Once sent, emails cannot be taken back and may later be used against a teacher by a disgruntled student. Teachers should never post a message or write an email to a student when they are angry, or write an email or message that they would not want the world to know about. It is also wise not to delete student emails but archive them for possible future reference.

The major complaint of online students is that professors do not reply quickly enough to their emails. On the one hand, many students believe that instructors are available around the clock and often want and expect immediate feedback. On the other hand, students often cannot proceed with their work until they receive an answer to their question. Although it seems reasonable to respond to student emails within twenty-four hours, instructors away at conferences, or out of town on holiday weekends, cannot always quickly return students emails. It is best to make it clear at the beginning of the semester that when possible the teacher will respond to students within twenty-four hours, and when the teacher is away it is best to put an announcement on the course site informing the students how long the teacher will be unavailable. When an assignment is due, however, an instructor should look at their email on a more regular basis to answer student problems.

There are many ways to limit the number of student emails sent to instructors In the first place. Some instructors advise students from the start that they will only respond to emails on certain days and at certain times, and will only address certain questions in their office hours, or at other pre-arranged meetings. Instructors can head off excessive email queries more successfully by making the syllabus and assignment instructions very clear and precise. In a traditional classroom it is easier for a teacher to explain an assignment and a student to ask a question if he or she does not understand. In an online class, unclear instructions will lead to an avalanche of emails to the instructor. Providing technical help, a course discussion forum for frequently asked questions and a list of commonly asked questions pertaining to navigation of the CMS will all lessen the need to contact the professor (see Box 5.1). In general, however, instructors have to spend more time answering emails from students in an online class than a traditional one. Students in a traditional classroom can ask questions before, during and after class. Without this avenue, online students email the instructor far more often to discuss course content.

Netiquette

Written communication among the students on discussion boards can also cause problems. In a history course, students often contribute to discussions on controversial and passionate topics with other students that they never see. Sometimes this communication can border on the offensive or inappropriate. A section on netiquette in the syllabus will remind students about acceptable online behavior and aid the elimination of these problems (see Box 5.2). A social discussion board used at the beginning of the semester will help to break down unfamiliarity among students. If an inappropriate posting does occur, teachers should take action by deleting the offending posting and reminding the students about netiquette.

Technical problems

Another possible source of tension between the teacher and the students concerns technical difficulties. Instructors need to be patient and flexible to technological problems that can affect the whole class, such as when a network server is down, and to technical issues that can affect individual students, such as when a computer is infected by a virus or a hard drive crashes. Neighborhoods can have power outages, quizzes can time out for no apparent reason, Internet links can disappear, and sending essays to the course site can often be a problem to some students. There is nothing more exasperating for a student than to settle

Box 5.1 Commonly asked questions

How do I ...?

- **How to post to a discussion forum (board)**: Step-by-step tutorial for posting to a discussion forum in ANGEL.

- **How to submit an assignment to a drop box**: tutorial for submitting an assignment to the drop box in ANGEL.

- **How to take an exam**: Instructions and guidelines for taking a test in ANGEL.

- **How do I view my grades?** Instructions for creating a grade report in ANGEL that can be run and saved for future use.

- **How to use ANGEL course mail (email):** The ANGEL course mail tool allows students and instructors to correspond with each other without requiring the use of an Internet email account.

- **How to forward ANGEL course mail to another email account**: Instructions for automatically forwarding ANGEL course mail to an Internet email account.

- **How to Post to a Live Chat**

- **How do I use ANGEL?** Click this link to view information about the various areas in ANGEL.

- **Print a PowerPoint presentation**: Step by step tutorial for students wanting to print multiple slides on one page.

- **Copying/pasting from Microsoft Word into the ANGEL text box**: Instructions for copying text written in Microsoft Word into the ANGEL textbox.

- **Search the Web**: A brief overview of how Internet search engines work and some tips for using them more efficiently.

- **Save documents that my instructor can open**: A step-by-step tutorial covering how to save word processor documents as rich text (.rtf) files for greater portability and accessibility.

- **Take a test using a dial-up connection**: Suggestions as to how students using dial-up connections can prevent being "timed out" by their Internet service provider and what to do if they are.

Source: Provided by the Joliet Junior College Distance Education Department.

Box 5.2 Netiquette guidelines

Students are expected to follow rules of etiquette, or netiquette, when posting online, and this contributes to more enjoyable and productive communication. The following tips for sending email and posting discussion board messages are adapted from guidelines originally compiled by Chuq Von Rospach and Gene Spafford (for complete guidelines see www.livinginternet.com/i/ia_nq_info_news.htm):

1 Never forget that the person on the other side is a human being who deserves courtesy and respect.

2 Be brief; succinct messages have the greatest impact.

3 Your messages reflect on YOU; take time to make sure that you are proud of them.

4 Use descriptive subject headings in your messages.

5 Think about your audience and stay on topic.

6 Be careful with humor and avoid sarcasm.

7 When you are making a follow-up comment to someone else's message, be sure to summarize the parts of the message to which you are responding.

8 Avoid repeating what has already been said.

9 Cite appropriate references whenever using someone else's ideas or words.

down for work and find they cannot perform the assigned task. It is also worth remembering that many of today's younger students are familiar with computers and with technology in general, but many other online learners are returning students who are less comfortable with technology.

There are many ways to alleviate the stress associated with technical problems. The college must make sure that technical help is always available. Instructors should not assign a lot of work on the automated testing part of the course site because online activity can easily be interrupted by technical problems with the server, or the computer. If the server goes down on the evening that a major assignment is due, teachers have to be prepared to extend their deadlines and keep students informed of developments (see Box 5.3). The students need to be responsible as well, however. Teachers should let students know that they need to keep backup copies of their work and that they should leave a telephone message at the instructor's office if they have computer difficulties. When a student insists that they sent a non-delivered email, the instructor can ask the student to retrieve the original email from the "sent" box and resend it.

Box 5.3 Course announcement regarding technical problems

SUNDAY, OCTOBER 31, 2004—TECHNICAL DIFFICULTIES

As many of you are aware, we are facing major technical difficulties with the Blackboard site. We have no twenty-four-hour backup technical service so I will have to wait until tomorrow (Monday) to speak to the site technician. I am extremely sorry for the inconvenience this is causing you; it is extremely frustrating. I will extend the deadline for the exam and the quizzes and will give you more information as soon as I get it tomorrow.

MONDAY, NOVEMBER 1, 2004—UP AND RUNNING!

I apologize once again about the technical difficulties that you experienced on Sunday. The good news is that the Blackboard site is up and running again. I have extended the deadline for Quiz 8 and Exam 2 until Tuesday evening (midnight) and reposted Quiz 8, Exam 2 essay questions, and Exam 2 fill-in-the-blank questions in the Assignments part of the course. All those that had technical problems please try to take them again. If you have any questions, email me and I will look at my email this evening and tomorrow morning.

Absenteeism

Even in an online class, students can be absent. The lack of classroom meetings and personal contact with the instructor can make some students procrastinate or forget to do their work. To avoid this, instructors should post an announcement every week to tell students what assignments they should have finished and what they should be doing this week. In addition, teachers can send an email reminder to those students who have not accessed the course or have not handed in an assessment and ask the students if they have any concerns. These emails should be encouraging and supportive and designed to motivate students, not to reprimand them.

The online student

Students often turn to inappropriate behavior because they are frustrated with the online experience. Most of the same student characteristics are needed for success in the online and the traditional classroom. Students need to be confident, motivated, and well organized. However, online students, who work alone a lot more and have less direct contact with, or constant help from, the instructor, require these in greater measure. The online environment can be socially isolating and online students have more opportunity to procrastinate. Those who are self-motivated, and who prefer to work alone, will do well in an online course; those who are not will struggle. Struggling students often turn their anger against the instructor, declaring that they are the victim of an instructor who is not doing enough teaching and letting the students do all the work. Problems with technology and the frustrations associated with communicating in writing are added factors in causing student stress in an online class.

To alleviate this stress, students require the help of the instructor and their educational institution. Assignments need to be engaging, and interaction with other students and frequent contact with the instructor encouraged. Students need encouragement from the instructor to motivate them and clear and consistent deadlines to help them to schedule their learning. Unclear assignments, poor instructions and directions, and disorganized course sites all irritate online students. Patience, flexibility, and empathy on behalf of the instructor are required to further ease behavioral problems. Offline backup for students also needs to be available. At a minimum, students require assistance with technical problems, access to computer labs on campus, academic help, and the availability of counselors.

In the end, academic dishonesty and other behavioral problems can be alleviated if not eliminated in an online class. Even in traditional classes instructors can never sure who has actually written the research papers that students produce at home. Both face-to-face and online instructors need to maintain good teacher-to-student interaction and to ease and manage student stress. We as teachers need to be careful about our online communication with our students, both in the discussion board and in email. Emails are very impersonal and can often be misunderstood. Finally, we need to consider the frustrations experienced by our students. Technology can often be exasperating for students and the online environment can be socially isolating. These both contribute towards friction between the teacher and the students.

Further reading

Beck, Evelyn and Donald Greive (2005) *Going the Distance: A Handbook for Part-Time and Adjunct Faculty Who Teach Online,* Ann Arbor MI: Adjunct Advocate. Evelyn Beck and Donald Greive provide some excellent suggestions on how to avoid plagiarism.

Engvig, Mona (2006) *Online Learning: All You Need to Know to Facilitate and Administer Online Courses,* Cresskill NJ: Hampton Press. This book pays particular attention to the students' views and perspective on online learning.

Ko, Susan and Steve Rossen (2004) *Teaching Online: A Practical Guide,* New York: Houghton Mifflin, second edition. This book is an excellent introduction to teaching online and includes plenty of indispensable information on classroom management.

Lewis, Chad (2000) "Taming the Lions and Tigers and Bears: The WRITE WAY to communicate online" in Ken W. White and Bob H. Weight (eds), *The Online Teaching Guide: A Handbook of Attitudes, Strategies, and Techniques for the Virtual Classroom,* Boston MA: Allyn & Bacon: 13–23. Lewis provides some excellent advice on online communication.

Palloff, Rena M. and Keith Pratt (2003) *The Virtual Student: A Profile and Guide to Working with Online Learners,* San Francisco CA, Jossey-Bass. This book helps instructors to understand the online student and suggests a number of ways to engage them in the online environment.

Priest, Lorraine (2000) "The Story of One Learner: A Student's Perspective on Online Teaching" in Ken W. White and Bob H. Weight (eds), *The Online Teaching Guide: A Handbook of Attitudes, Strategies, and Techniques for the Virtual Classroom,* Boston MA: Allyn & Bacon: 37–44. Online instructors need to understand the online experience from the students' perspective. Yet the vast majority of articles on online learning have been written by instructors and we have little from the online student. An exception is this fine article by Lorraine Priest.

Varvel Jr, Virgil E. (2005) "Honesty in Online Education," *Pointers and Clickers* 6. Accessed June 15, 2008 at: www.ion.illinois.edu/resources/pointersclickers/2005_ 01/VarvelCheatPoint2005.pdf. Virgil Varvel argues that the anonymity of the online environment, and the physical separation between instructor and student, can lead to problems with academic dishonesty. Varvel suggests a number of strategies to overcome some of these problems.

White, Ken (2000) "Dealing With Challenging Situations: Communicating Through Online Conflict" in Ken W. White and Bob H. Weight (eds), *The Online Teaching Guide: A Handbook of Attitudes, Strategies, and Techniques for the Virtual Classroom,* Boston MA: Allyn and Bacon: 142–54. White suggests that online conflict offers a learning opportunity and he provides a number of useful tips on how instructors should respond to online conflict.

Online teaching in the face-to-face classroom

IN THE TWENTY-FIRST CENTURY, computer technology has not only introduced a whole new teaching environment, the online classroom, it has also launched a new type of course, the blended or hybrid class, and transformed how we can teach face-to-face classes. In a blended or hybrid class, which combines traditional face-to-face teaching with online learning, classroom time is reduced, but not eliminated, and a substantial proportion of the content is replaced by online activities. In contrast, in a traditional face-to-face class that incorporates online components, the classroom remains the main focus of teaching. In both cases, the use of the CMS allows instructors to extend learning beyond the classroom walls and provide students with a greater variety, and often far superior, resources to work with.

Advantages of a blended class

A blended class has major advantages over a strictly face-to-face class. Online learning provides multimedia technologies to engage students, to encourage student-centered learning and to reach all learning styles. The World Wide Web provides students with multiple resources to study history. There is increased communication and collaboration among students and between students and instructor. Students can participate in blogs, wikis and online discussion boards at any time. Rather than wait for the instructors' office hours or the next class meeting to ask a question or provide an opinion, students can use online communication tools to carry on a discussion with the instructor.

If blended classes offer advantages over a traditional course, they also provide a number of benefits over a class taught purely online. The exciting interactive lectures and dynamic discussions of a traditional classroom simply cannot be replicated online. Meeting in the traditional classroom allows online students to break out of the social isolation of the online environment. The traditional element of a blended class makes the students feel more connected, as they can see, and informally talk to, their peers in the classroom. The real human element of conversing with students, getting to know them, and having humorous asides are the enjoyable part of classroom teaching for instructors and students alike.

Disadvantages of a blended class

For all of these advantages, blended classes have their problems. A recent report by the Sloan foundation found that offerings of blended courses in the US decreased between 2003 and 2005, while online course offerings grew. Only 38 percent of respondents agreed that "Blended courses hold more promise than online courses."[13] Much of the problem stems from the fact that students are uncertain about the nature and value of blended classes. Students who have enrolled in blended classes often complain that they find it difficult to adapt to both environments. They do not really know what enrolling in a blended class entails, and some are surprised that they have to do a lot of work online. In contrast, other students think that the on-campus part of a blended class is not as important as the online part. Some students say "Why have class time at all when assignments and assessments can be undertaken online?" As a result, absenteeism from campus is a major problem with blended classes.

Blended courses have their drawbacks for instructors, too. Many instructors admit that they find it difficult to divide up the tasks between the classroom and the online environment. There is often not enough time to complete substantial class activities in the shortened class sessions. Subjects with strong practical elements, such as speech, nursing or science classes that require laboratory work, cannot be taught solely online and seem to require an on-campus element to them. Those subjects without a practical element to them, such as history, seem more suited to the online environment than the blended one.

Teaching a blended class

Because of these problems, a blended course must be well organized. Instructors have to guide students through a type of course that students probably know little about. On the first day of class, instructors should discuss the types of learning activities performed in the course so that students are aware of what they are getting into prior to the start of the course. Instructors may want to impress on to students the importance of both parts of the class, campus and online, and let the students know that it is important to attend on campus. A significant portion of the first class should also involve a thorough demonstration of the features in the CMS used in the course.

Blended classes can take different forms. The spine or backbone of a blended course could be the online element and classroom time can then be built around preparatory or explanatory work. In this way, the traditional classroom can be used for the personal touch of teacher-to-student interaction, whether in the form of a lecture, question and answer sessions, the summation of the previous week's work or the introduction of new material. The technology of the online environment could be used for collaborative work and for completing assignments. Students could then report back to class on their findings and gain feedback from the other students and the instructor. Conversely, assignments could be distributed across both the face-to-face and the online areas of the class. Students could answer different questions on the same topic within the online discussion board and then bring their ideas into class to discuss. Alternatively, students could use computers in a conventional classroom setting with the instructor at hand to coordinate activities.

Another option is for the instructor to organize activities in the traditional classroom that are difficult to organize online. The face-to-face part of a blended class can include student presentations and group projects. Time in the face-to-face classroom could be used for groups to meet and for student presentations. Exams are problematic online because of worries about cheating, so class time could be used for taking exams and other graded activities.

Integrating online teaching into the traditional classroom

For all the benefits of blended classes, more and more face-to-face courses are using online elements, and the distinction between campus-based traditional classes and blended classes has blurred. Moreover, many of the benefits of a blended class can be achieved in a Web-assisted traditional class or one that uses a CMS. To illustrate this point, I will describe how I redesigned my undergraduate "World History Since 1500" face-to-face course to incorporate a number of online elements.

"World History Since 1500" course

"World History Since 1500" is the second part of a two-semester survey course of world history that I have taught since Fall 2001. The course chronologically examines different themes, which together create an overview of the evolving structure of world society between 1500 and the present. Through a variety of historical sources the course sets out to understand how the world that was so disparate and separate in 1500 became so interlocked and dependent in the next 500 years. This approach looks at global trends such as colonization, industrialization and immigration, and how specific countries dealt with these developments and in the process developed closer ties with one another. At the end of the course, the successful student should be able to:

- identify the main figures, forces and events in world history since 1500;
- analyze and describe the cultural, economic, political and technological developments since 1500 that have led to the development of an interconnected world;
- analyze primary sources;
- evaluate historical arguments;
- create historical arguments in a variety of written forms;
- display an ability to undertake original historical research.

When I originally designed the class, I set out to elicit student outcomes with interesting assignments and readings. The assigned readings were a textbook with a strong narrative structure, Peter N. Stearns, *World History In Brief: Major Patterns of Change and Continuity*, and a historical novel or biographical study. To improve their reading, writing, and critical thinking skills, students had to write 250-word papers each week based on the assigned readings. They also completed a total of seven quizzes during the semester. The quizzes were centered on objective questions from the lectures and classroom handouts and helped the students identify the main figures, forces and events in world history and the cultural, economic, political and technological developments in the world since 1500. The students also had to take three essay exams: two mid-terms and a final exam. All helped the students to formulate historical arguments. They also had to write two six-page papers: an essay on an assigned book or history website of their choosing and an oral history paper in which the students had to interview their oldest living relative about their role in recent world events. The classroom activities featured interactive lectures, discussion, and small group activities, all of which improve students speaking and critical thinking skills.

I have slowly introduced technology into the world history classroom. At first, the only technology I used in the classroom was an overhead projector, a videocassette recorder and a portable stereo system to play music. I subsequently embraced email and PowerPoint. Initially I only used a CMS in my online classes, but once I saw the benefits that some of the CMS tools could bring to my classroom teaching I gradually began to incorporate online components into my traditional classes.

Faculty information

The CMS can be a great supplement to the face-to-face class and, surprisingly, can help students establish a personal relationship with the instructor. We spend very little time introducing ourselves to our students in a traditional classroom, mainly because of a lack of time, but students should be able to know a little about the person who is teaching the class. A CMS allows the teacher to post faculty information and let the students know more about the professional and personal background of the instructor. Alongside information about office hours and contact information, instructors can post a CV, a list of publications, details of research and teaching interests, and biographical information. The instructor should make sure that they tailor the biographical information to suit the course they are teaching. Travels in Latin America are more relevant to a Latin American history class than a British history course. Similarly, originating in England is more relevant in a British history class than a US one. With this information, students can understand the instructors' perspective on history and teaching, appreciate their academic experience and develop a more personal connection to them, and some students may even be inspired to pursue history as a career (see Figure 6.1).

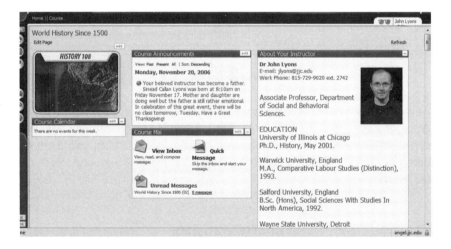

Figure 6.1 Faculty information and course announcement

Announcements page

The ability to post announcements on the CMS is also valuable for the face-to-face class. The announcements page keeps students abreast of all course developments. It can remind students of assignment deadlines or upcoming events in class or on campus. The announcements page can convey important information that only became apparent to the instructor between classes. If the instructor unexpectedly cannot make it to class, for example, an announcement can alert the students and save them a wasted and frustrating trip to campus. This area can also be used to highlight an important point made in the classroom or to bring closure to an activity that was left unfinished in class (see Figure 6.1).

Online quizzes

The ability to provide online quizzes is another feature of a CMS that I incorporated into the traditional classroom. I replaced the seven in-class quizzes with weekly timed multiple choice online quizzes based on information from the textbook. The students have to take the quizzes before they come to class, which encourages them to read and be prepared for a class discussion of the material. Valuable classroom time can now be spent on teaching rather than on test taking, and when students come to class I can be sure that they have completed the required reading ready for class discussion.

Grade book

The grade book function in the CMS is useful to students and to the instructor. The grade book keeps students up to date with their progress in the class. For instructors it eliminates the tiresome practice of manually adding up the grades at the end of the semester, and it stops students constantly asking teachers for their grade.

Course statistics

One CMS function that instructors often overlook is the "Course Statistics" area. This generates reports on course activity. Instructors can see when, and if, a specific student accessed the course site, and what area of the course they viewed. This function is particularly useful in a face-to-face class. Instructors can tell if a student logged into the course to view an assigned reading for a class discussion. It is also possible to see how often a student participated in

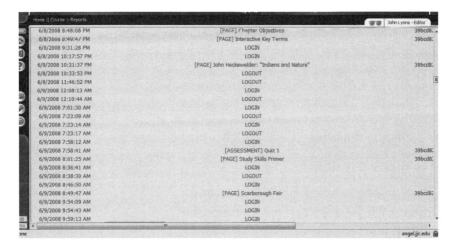

Figure 6.2 Course statistics

Note: Students' names have been shaded out of this figure to preserve anonymity.

an online group activity. Alternatively, "Course Statistics" can be used by the instructor to check whether a student logged on to the course site to take a timed quiz that the student has insisted was not visible on their computer (see Figure 6.2).

Discussion board

So far, the most successful attempt to incorporate elements of online teaching into my world history class has been the use of the online discussion board. Class periods are a combination of lecture and discussion with the discussions based on the textbook and other readings. Before I used a CMS, it was clear that many students did not read the assigned texts and were unprepared for class discussion. Now I assign online discussion questions before class, which promotes discussion of course material outside of class and in the face-to-face classroom. Students are more confident to speak in class if they have already put their thoughts together in an online discussion. They are not faced with having to come up with spontaneous answers to questions asked in the classroom. I post a discussion question each week to replace the weekly essays I previously assigned. A minimum of three weekly postings is required to receive maximum credit for participation. Students seem more interested in an online discussion than an essay assignment and they also gain feedback from their peers.

The discussion questions focus on a number of different sources. Some questions center on the student's oral history project. Other questions are based on online readings, websites, music or paintings. I also include discussion questions that focus on lectures in the classroom. I post a question after class that asks students what they learned from the day's class. Subsequently, I sometimes tailor the activities in the classroom to fill in gaps in the students' knowledge evidenced by a close reading of the discussion board.

The discussion board could also be used as a forum for study groups. On many campuses, students want to study with other students but find it difficult to coordinate conflicting schedules. The instructor could break the class into smaller groups that could use the discussion board to discuss classroom activities or to study for exams.

Online resource center

The ability to post course material via website links or by attachments also permits me to use the CMS as a repository of information. I add different folders in an area of the CMS I have entitled the "resource center", with each folder containing information related to course topics. I've attached word documents that contain lists of history books, historical novels, ethnic restaurants and films on historical topics into this reference area of the CMS. Study guides, class handouts, and rubrics are also included in the resource center. I've added music, links to websites and databases, and PowerPoint presentations that I have shown in class (see Figure 6.3).

The online resource center has many uses. I play the music and view the websites in the classroom. Students use the resources for term papers, projects and other assignments. Instead of putting articles on reserve at the library, most of which are checked out the day before an assignment is due, students can access the articles online. The intrepid student can use the resources to further their knowledge of a historical topic outside of the class. Instructors can post their lecture notes, PowerPoint presentations or podcasts online after class, for those students who missed the lecture, or for those who want to review it again. Alternatively, lectures can be posted before class and the students can discuss the lecture topic in the classroom.

The podcasting of lectures is increasingly popular, but classroom lectures are not really suited for podcasts. With the lecturer having control of the microphone, it is often impossible to hear student questions or comments and therefore podcasts tend to reinforce the non-interactive lecture style. To capture the interactive nature of a lecture/discussion, instructors would need multiple microphones in the classroom. If an instructor podcasts his or her lecture there is also the possibility that students will no longer turn up for class.

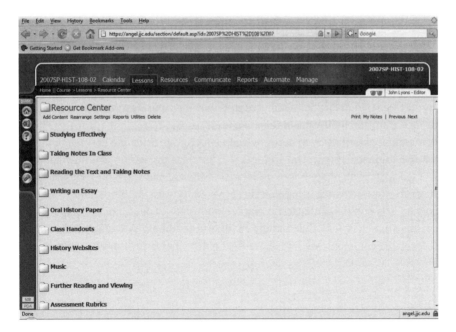

Figure 6.3 Course resource center

Paperless classroom

For the environmentally conscious, the CMS allows the creation of a paperless classroom. Syllabus, study guides, exams and class handouts can be posted online and be available twenty-four hours a day. A lost syllabus or study guide is no longer an excuse for missing an assignment. Students who have lost their syllabus or misplaced a guide to an assignment can now immediately obtain them from the CMS. Essay assignments can be submitted, graded and returned via the CMS. In effect, all graded activities can take place online, freeing up more class time for other activities.

It is possible to go completely paperless and entirely do away with assigned books. The *Internet History Sourcebooks Project*, at www.fordham.edu/halsall, provides an extensive collection of public domain and copy-permitted historical texts. Many history books are now available online. Public domain texts are available at www.gutenberg.org, for example. *Google Book Search* also has full texts of books online, and the site allows searches of the books stored in the digital database.

Online activities

When I introduced a CMS into my "World History Since 1500" class, I made some changes to my prevailing teaching methods (see Box 6.1 for an example). Indeed, with the introduction of online elements into my world history class, an ideal learning environment is created that incorporates the best from face-to-face traditional classroom teaching and the best from online learning. I can now choose activities from both environments that provide the optimal outcome for the students. Interactive lectures and in-class discussion are now complemented with technology-based assignments that fit the learning styles of more students. Assignments using collaborative tools such as blogs and wikis are particularly popular. Interactive maps, simulations, videos, podcasts and music engage students more than simply reading a textbook. A CMS, which allows students to communicate and share files online, helps with group projects.

Box 6.1 Lesson plan: industrialization

A wonderful activity for my world history class involves using the US Historical Census Browser created by the Inter-University Consortium for Political and Social Research and available from the University of Virginia, Geospatial and Statistical Data Center: http://fisher.lib.virginia.edu/collections/stats/histcensus. The data is drawn from every state and county in the US from 1790 to 1970. The browser allows students to examine multiple topics such as education and literacy, the economy, ethnicity, race, agriculture and slave population. It is possible to view the data over time in the form of tables and interactive maps. Students can simply click on a year and category to retrieve the information they need.

I use this data to let students discuss economic changes in their own region and in the nation in general. On the class discussion board, students answer the following questions: "Using the data you have collected, how did Will County change in the nineteenth century? Did these changes reflect national changes? Explain these trends." Alternatively, students can compare the changes that occurred in two US states during the twentieth century. The conversation then moves into the face-to-face classroom and opens into a more general discussion about the changes brought by industrialization.

Student responses

How do the students in my "World History Since 1500" course respond to taking a class with so many online elements? The students dislike doing online quizzes based on the textbook, but no more than they would dislike in-class quizzes. Conversely, I really think instructors will see an improvement in class discussion when students are forced to read the text through regular quizzing. Students like to use the discussion board because it deepens relationships among students between classes. The immediate availability of quiz grades, the enhanced communication offered by the announcements page, and the accessibility of the grade book are enthusiastically received by the students. Podcasts are also very popular among the technologically proficient students.

Graduate tutorials and seminars

Although the class I discuss above is an undergraduate class, some of the ideas can be incorporated into graduate discussion classes. Faculty information, announcements, the grade book and course statistics can play the same role in a graduate class as they do in an undergraduate one. The online resource center can provide links to many databases of online journals, which are the cornerstone of a graduate seminar. Making sure that students do the reading is probably more important in a graduate class, where discussion, rather than lecture, often dominates. The online quizzes are an obvious way to encourage reading and provide the added bonus of automatic grading.

The discussion board can also be successfully incorporated into a graduate class. Students can carry on a discussion of an assigned book or article outside of class, with the conversation flowing from the face-to-face classroom to the online environment. Alternatively, the instructor could open an online book club. Each student is then asked to write a book review that other students have to respond to. Another idea is to ask one student each week to lead an online discussion on a reading or historiographical topic. This way the student, not the instructor, chooses a topic for discussion, gathers the readings, designs the questions, and facilitates the discussion.

Other online tools could be utilized to great effect in a graduate class. Peer review of student papers posted online would seem most appropriate for the graduate classroom. Each student could review a recently published book on a blog and open a dialogue with students within the class or with those at other institutions. Podcasts that feature interviews with historians would seem to be useful here. Or even better, Skype could be used to interview the authors of assigned books and provide an opportunity for the students to discuss the book with the author. Students could use wikis or social bookmarking to build and share annotated bibliographies.

Initially, I used a CMS only in my online classes, but once I saw the improvements that some of the CMS functions could bring to my teaching I incorporated a CMS into my traditional classes. CMSs augment what is done in the classroom and extend the classroom in time and space beyond the classroom walls. The grade book keeps students up to date with their progress in the class and for instructors it eliminates the end of semester practice of manually adding up the grades. The faculty information on the CMS helps break down the mystique surrounding the professor and personalize the student–instructor relationship a little more. Quizzes and exams can be taken online, freeing up classroom time for other activities, and quizzes are automatically graded by the computer. Students can more easily communicate with their instructors and their fellow students between classes either in the discussion board or by email. The announcements page and email allow faculty to communicate with students in between classes. The CMS can also be used as a reference area that builds up a list of websites, books, music and articles, which can all be incorporated into the classroom or used for homework assignments. It is possible to create a paperless classroom in which the syllabus, study guides and handouts are available to students at any time. The online elements can be a supplement to our instruction and can even change how we teach a class. Online learning can transform the face-to-face classroom by making constructivist, collaborative and student-centered pedagogy easier to adopt. Introducing CMSs into a traditional class can enhance the educational experience for the students and the instructor.

Further reading

Cantu, D. Antonio and Wilson J. Warren (2003) *Teaching History in the Digital Classroom* (New York: M. E. Sharpe). Cantu and Warren describe how to incorporate technology into the curriculum, describing lesson plans, instructional models and assessment strategies. Most chapters in this book offer ideas on using technology in the traditional face-to-face classroom but some of the ideas can be adapted to the blended environment.

Creed, Tom (1997) "Extending the Classroom Walls Electronically" in William E. Campbell and Karl A. Smith (eds) *New Paradigms for College Teaching,* Edina MN: Interaction Book Co. One of the first, and still most insightful, articles on using online technology in the classroom.

Garrison, D. Randy and Heather Kanuka (2004) "Blended Learning: Uncovering its Transformative Potential in Higher Education," *The Internet and Higher Education* 7. This article discusses the educational benefits of blended learning and argues for the need for institutional support for both students and teachers.

Hijazi, Sam, M. Crowley, M. Leigh Smith and C. Shaffer (2006) "Maximizing Learning by Teaching Blended Courses," Accessed June 15, 2008 at: http://fits.depauw.edu/ascue/proceedings/2006/Papers/p67.pdf. A wide-ranging article that discusses the planning and the design of a blended course. The authors provide suggestions for adopting components from traditional and online learning.

Minielli, Maureen C. and S. Pixy Ferris (September 2005) "Electronic Courseware in Higher Education," *First Monday* 10. Accessed June 15, 2008 at: http://firstmonday. org/issues/issue10_9/minielli/index.html. This article examines how to effectively utilize a CMS in the classroom and urges educators to rethink existing practices.

Ullman, Craig and Mitchell Rabinowitz (October 2004) "Course Management Systems and the Reinvention of Instruction," *The Journal*. Accessed June 15, 2008 at: http://thejournal.com/articles/17014_1. Craig Ullman and Mitchell Rabinowitz argue that there can be a "reinvention of instruction" with the use of a CMS in a traditional class. They suggest that class time should be almost exclusively devoted to discussion and student activities.

Conclusion

MORE AND MORE HISTORY instructors are being asked to teach online courses. Yet many fear that with the huge amount of course preparation, the lack of face-to-face contact, the intensive use of discussion boards, and the constant emailing of students that they will spend more of their time teaching online courses than traditional ones and with less rewarding results for both teacher and students. There certainly are many challenges in providing a history course online, but a well-designed and administered course can alleviate the demands on teachers and produce an exciting and gratifying learning experience for students. What is a well-designed and administered online course?

- The course should be student centered. The students must be encouraged to work with the multiple history resources available on the World Wide Web, to utilize some of the many online learning tools, and to engage in varied forms of assessments. The online environment is ideal for facilitating active learning, letting students pursue their own interests, and meeting all learning styles.
- The instructor needs to encourage student-to-student collaboration. By organizing collaborative activities among online students, students break free of the social isolation experienced online and contribute to the knowledge sharing taking place.
- Although online methods change teaching, traditional teaching qualities and techniques still remain important. Instructors need a strong grasp of the subject matter, to hold the students to high standards, a passion for teaching and learning, good organizational skills and a caring approach to those they teach.
- Teacher-to-student communication is vital for student success. Teachers must personalize the online experience and provide frequent feedback and encouragement to the students.

- The course requires substantial offline backup for students. Students often become distracted, disheartened or frustrated when taking online courses, partly because of the lack of assistance offline. An online orientation ought to be required and technical help, counseling and academic assistance readily available.
- There is no need to completely abandon the face-to-face classroom for the online environment. The best of online elements such as the discussion board and interactive technology can be added to the dynamic nature of the traditional classroom.

While the online environment is an excellent place for learning, instructors can only take full advantage of the opportunities afforded by online learning by constantly re-evaluating and improving their teaching. Online learning is evolving at a rapid pace and to keep an online course up to date with innovations in teaching, technology, and the study of history is important. Educational theorists and practitioners are continuously providing new ways to think about teaching. New technology is constantly developing that can make some of our teaching practices outmoded. History books pour off the presses offering new perspectives on standard topics and new areas of study.

There are many ways to remain current with innovations in teaching history online. While journal articles and books can often be out of date by the time they are published, websites, blogs, and podcasts often provide the most current educational research, techniques, and opinions and are the best way to keep up to date with the quickly changing world of online learning. Much can also be gained from reading longer research articles from traditional sources of information. In addition to reading books and journals that focus on online learning and on the historical subjects they teach, instructors can subscribe to journals devoted to the teaching of history.

Continued improvement can also come from discussing online learning with other instructors and with online students. Talk to other teachers about their online experiences and find out what did, and did not, work for them. Instructors should ask colleagues to evaluate their course site and do the same for them. Find out from students what online classes they enjoyed and what they particularly liked about those classes. Together with the distance education department, organize regular meetings on campus to discuss online teaching strategies and invite guest speakers to talk to the college community. Attend workshops and academic conferences on online learning. Instructors can find upcoming conferences in education and educational technology by viewing *Teaching and Learning Conferences Worldwide* at www.conferencealerts.com/school.htm and *E-learning Conferences Worldwide* at www.conferencealerts.com/elearning.htm.

It is an exciting time to be an online history teacher. Online instructors are pioneering a new way of teaching, one that is constantly changing and evolving. Yet many of the attributes of a good teacher remain the same whether we teach in a face-to-face classroom or an online one. In the end, I hope this book encourages instructors to experiment with new technologies and new teaching strategies but also to merge them with traditional teaching virtues and methods.

Sample syllabus

HISTORY OF THE UNITED STATES TO 1865

Fall 2008
Course Number: HIST 103-W1
Credit Hours: 3
Prerequisites: Prior to the start of the course, students must have successfully completed the online orientation.

Instructor contact information

Instructor: Dr John Lyons
Office: J-4023 Main Campus
Office hours: Monday to Friday 7:30–8:00am and 11:00am–noon
Telephone: (815) 280–2742
Email: jlyons@jjc.edu
Department   Social and Behavioral Sciences Department
  mailing   J-4002
  address: Joliet Junior College
                 1215 Houbolt Road
                 Joliet IL 60431
                 Department telephone: (815) 280–6634

Welcome to the course

This online class is designed for disciplined, self-motivated, independent learners. You are expected to spend nine to twelve hours per week completing readings and assignments for this course. You must have good writing and basic Internet and computer skills, and have access to a computer to successfully complete the course. You must back up your work and be able to use other computers, on campus or at your local public library, for example, if you are having problems with your computer. Each week we will be reading chapters of the textbook, taking quizzes based on the readings and participating in online discussions. We will also be analyzing primary sources, examining websites, watching videos and listening to music. Please consult the Course Schedule area of the syllabus and closely follow the weekly announcements on the course site for further information.

Although we will be moving through the semester as a class, there are times during the semester when you will be studying on your own. I am committed to being available to students throughout the semester by returning-emails within twenty-four hours and returning graded course work within a week. Students should access the course website and your JJC email account on a daily basis. Please post all questions about course content or assignments to the Question and Answer forum in the course site. Only email the instructor about confidential matters such as grades, etc. When you send me an email make sure you put your name and course number (HIST 103-W1) in the subject line of the email. Please use your college email account.

Course description (from college catalogue)

This course is a survey of the political, economic, social, religious and cultural developments of the United States from 1492 to 1865. Emphasis is on such topics as colonial society, the Revolution, the young republic, nationalism, expansionism, slavery, sectionalism and the Civil War.

Learning outcomes

The History of the United States to 1865 suggests that the US was created by the interaction of three racial groups: the indigenous people of North America; Western Europeans, particularly those originating from Great Britain; and the people of Africa. These three groups had different associations with one another and because of power relations did not play an equal role in determining the character of the new nation. This course explores the relations between the three and the character of the new nation they established. This course is built around the following question: What role did the indigenous people of North America, Europe and Africa play in United States history prior to 1865? The successful student will be able to:

- analyze and describe the role of the indigenous people of North America, Africa and Europe in US history to 1865;
- identify the main figures, forces and events in US history to 1865;
- analyze primary sources;
- evaluate historical arguments;
- create historical arguments in a variety of written forms;
- display an ability to undertake original historical research.

Required readings

1   James Davidson *et al. Nation of Nations: A Concise Narrative of the American Republic,* vol. 1, fourth edition.
2   Supplemental readings are provided in the Course Documents section of the course site. Please consult the Course Schedule area of the syllabus and closely follow the weekly announcements on the course site for further information.

Technical requirements

Internet access (56K modem minimum, broadband preferred); Windows OS: Microsoft Internet Explorer 6.0 or higher (recommended browser), and Firefox 1.5 or higher; Macintosh OS: Firefox 1.5 or higher, Safari is NOT supported at this time; Windows Media Player for audio files; and word processing (Microsoft Word strongly recommended).

Course requirements

1   Discussion board participation

Participation in the class's discussion board will count 150 points toward the final course grade and will be based on the quality and quantity of postings. I will post a new discussion question each Monday morning. A minimum of three weekly postings is required from you by the following Sunday evening to receive maximum credit for participation. The first posting should directly answer the discussion question and the next two should respond to other students' postings. Each posting should be a paragraph in length. The first posting should be at least 250 words long. My role as your instructor within the discussion forums is to facilitate discussion by providing probing questions, to keep the discussion on track and to help enforce etiquette. I will not respond to every post because I want you to share your thoughts and ideas with each other. I will, however, respond to the discussions in the announcements page at the end of the week and post an individual grade in the grade book. Please look at the discussion rubric and discussion board example posting in the Course Documents part of the course site before contributing to the discussion board.

2   14 weekly quizzes

The quizzes are multiple choice and are based on the chapters from James Davidson *et al. Nation of Nations.* The quizzes will cover the material listed under the week's reading except quiz 1, which will cover all of Chapter 1. Quizzes are posted on the Monday and must be taken by the following Sunday. You have ten minutes to take each quiz. The point of the quizzes is to encourage you to read the James Davidson *et al. Nation of Nations* textbook closely and to assess your knowledge of the text.

3   Video, PowerPoint or podcast presentation

The paper is due on Sunday October 19. For further information, please see the handout in the Course Documents part of the course site.

4   Three online exams in the form of essays

The exams are all essays, which will help you to develop your analytical and writing skills and allow you to create historical arguments. The exams are posted on the Monday morning and must be taken by the following Sunday evening. The exams are not timed, you can open and access them as many times as you like. You don't have to complete them in one sit-down session. For all essay assignments, please see the rubrics in the Course Documents part of the course site.

5   Local history paper

Write a paper that addresses the following question: What role did the local area play in the nation's history until 1865? This research paper allows you to demonstrate an ability to undertake original historical research. The paper should be double spaced and at least seven pages in length with an additional title page and bibliography. The paper is due on Sunday December 7. For further information, please see the handout in the Course Documents part of the course site.

6   Extra credit paper

Critically review one of the websites listed under Course Documents, History Websites, in a two-page double-spaced paper. The paper is due on Sunday December 7. For further information, please see the handout in the Course Documents part of the course site.

Graded course work

The following graded course work is assigned during the semester and will form the basis of final course grades:

Discussion participation	150 pts
Weekly quizzes	140 pts
Video, PowerPoint or podcast presentation	150 pts
2 online exams (100 pts each)	200 pts
Online final exam	160 pts
Local history paper	200 pts
Extra credit paper	20 pts.

Final course grades

Final grades are based on the student's accumulated points:

A   900–1,000 points
B   800–899 points
C   700–799 points
D   600–699 points
F   0–599 points.

Assignment deadlines

The due dates for each graded assignment can be found in the Course Schedule. The deadline for each assignment is midnight of the assigned day. All late assignments will receive zero points. If the assignment is late because of medical or other exceptional circumstances, the grade will be reduced by 10 percent per day it is late.

Question and answer forum

If you have any questions about course content or assignments that would be of interest to other students you can post them to the Question and Answer forum in the course site. If you know the answer to the student's question, please post a reply. Don't post anything here you don't want other students to read. Email the instructor about confidential matters such as grades, etc.

Lounge area

This is an informal discussion area for students. Here students can post on any subject that interests them. Students can discuss music, films, novels, etc. that they have enjoyed over the length of the semester.

Technical assistance

Do not contact the instructor about technical problems. For assistance with technical problems, contact the Support Center at www.jjc.edu/help or phone 1–866–361–8864. Technicians are available 24 hours a day, 7 days a week, 365 days a year. Face-to-face help is available in the Distance Education Technology Center for Teaching and Learning in Room J-4019 on the Main Campus from Monday through Thursday, 8am to 8pm, and on Fridays from 8am to 4:30pm.

Academic assistance

Students may wish to utilize the many services offered by the Academic Skills Center (ASC) (J2013-Main Campus). Some students, for example, may schedule appointments with tutors in the ASC, who are available at no cost to provide assistance. For more information call 815–280–2284.

Campus computer labs

Computers are available in the college library and computer labs. Assistants are available to answer questions. A JJC ID number is required to use these labs. For computer lab hours and more information, visit www.jjc.edu/academic computing or call (815) 729–9020, ext. 2637.

Writing Center

For writing assistance contact the Writing Center located in C-2001 on Main Campus. For more information or to set up an appointment, call (815) 280–2730.

Library

The Library is located on the third floor of J-Building on Main Campus. Phone numbers:

Circulation desk   (815) 280-BOOK (2665)
Reference desk   (815) 280–2344
Web address   www.jjc.edu/lrc

Special needs

Students with documented disabilities, including a learning disability, who require special accommodations, should contact me during the first week of the semester. Students requesting special needs must be registered with the Student Accommodations and Resources (STaR) program located in J-2009 on Main Campus. Phone: (815) 280–2613 or visit www.jjc.edu/star.

Withdrawal/drop policy

If a student determines that he/she will be unable to complete the course, it is the student's responsibility to officially withdraw from the course. Failure to officially withdraw will result in a failing (F) grade in the course. Contact the Registrar's Office at 815–744–2200 for further information on withdrawal procedures.

Incomplete grades

Incomplete (I) grades and deadline extensions are not options in this course. Students must complete their work before the deadlines outlined in the syllabus.

Netiquette

Students are expected to follow rules of etiquette, or netiquette, when posting online, and this contributes to more enjoyable and productive communication. The following tips for sending email and posting discussion board messages are adapted from guidelines originally compiled by Chuq Von Rospach and Gene Spafford. For complete guidelines see www.livinginternet.com/i/ia_nq_info_news.htm:

1 Never forget that the person on the other side is a human being who deserves courtesy and respect.
2 Be brief; succinct messages have the greatest impact.
3 Your messages reflect on YOU; take time to make sure that you are proud of them.
4 Use descriptive subject headings in your messages.
5 Think about your audience and stay on topic.
6 Be careful with humor and avoid sarcasm.
7 When you are making a follow-up comment to someone else's message, be sure to summarize the parts of the message to which you are responding.
8 Avoid repeating what has already been said.
9 Cite appropriate references whenever using someone else's ideas or words.

Acceptable use policy

Students are responsible for knowing and following the terms and conditions of JJC's Acceptable Use Policy for Information Technology. This policy may be found in the college catalog and student handbook, posted in computer labs on campus, at the student kiosks and online at www.jjc.edu/acadkemic computing.

Academic dishonesty

Joliet Junior College Student Handbook states that acts of academic dishonesty include "cheating which includes, but is not limited to: Use of any unauthorized assistance in taking quizzes, tests, or examinations." Plagiarism includes, but is not limited to: "The unacknowledged use of materials prepared by another person, or agency, or internet website, engaged in the selling of term papers or other academic materials" (155). Any student found cheating/plagiarizing will receive a fail for the work and may be dropped from the course.

Sexual harassment

The college has a clear and firm policy prohibiting sexual harassment. Even though this is an online class, sexual harassment can, nonetheless, occur. Such conduct will not be tolerated in this class, and victims are encouraged to report any unwelcome sexual advances to appropriate school authorities (see college catalog and/or student handbook). Learning is best achieved in an environment of mutual respect and trust.

Course schedule

Module 1

Week 1 (August 25): Introduction

Discussion Question 1: Why do we study history? What figure in US history do you most admire and why?

Readings: Davidson, *Global Essay: The Creation of a New America,* pp. xlviii–3.

Week 2 (September 1): The indigenous people of the Americas

Discussion Question 2: Go to Lessons, Course Documents, PowerPoint Presentations, and view the Indigenous People of North America presentation. After viewing the presentation, what similarities and differences do you see in the lives of the indigenous people of North America?

Readings: Davidson, Chapter 1, pp. 10–14.

View: Indigenous People of North America PowerPoint presentation.

Week 3 (September 8): Europeans

Discussion Question 3: Go to Lessons, Course Documents, Primary Sources, Indigenous People of North America and read the article "Indians and Nature" by John Heckewelder. According to John Heckewelder, what were the Indians views of nature, religion, and property? How accurate do you think his views were?

Readings: Davidson, Chapter 1, pp. 4–10 and 14–32 and John Heckewelder "Indians and Nature."

Quiz 1: Chapter 1.

Week 4 (September 15): Settlement in the Colonial South, 1600–1750

Discussion Question 4: Go to Lessons, Course Documents, History Websites, Settlement in the Colonial South, view the websites on the Jamestown colony and answer the following question: What do the websites on the Jamestown settlement tell you about life in the colonial South? Give specific examples.

Readings: Davidson, Chapter 2.

View: Websites on the Jamestown settlement.

Quiz 2: Chapter 2.

Week 5 (September 22): Settlement in the Colonial North, 1600–1700

Readings: Davidson, Chapter 3.
Quiz 3: Chapter 3.
Exam 1: Due Sunday September 28

Module 2

Week 6 (September 29): Eighteenth-century America

Discussion Question 5: Go to Lessons, Course Documents, Music, and play music selections 1 to 5 and answer the following questions: How did the music of the Native Americans, Africans and Europeans differ? What role/purpose did music play for each group in early American history?
Readings: Davidson, Chapter 4.
Listen: Musical selections 1 to 5.
Quiz 4: Chapter 4

Week 7 (October 6): Toward the War for American Independence, 1754–1776

Discussion Question 6: Go to Lessons, Course Documents, PowerPoint Presentations, Boston Massacre, view Paul Revere's Engraving of the Boston Massacre and answer the following questions: In what specific ways is Revere's print inaccurate? Why exactly did Revere make these inaccurate depictions? Was the "Boston Massacre" really a "Massacre"?
Readings: Davidson, Chapter 5.
View: Boston Massacre PowerPoint presentation.
Quiz 5: Chapter 5.

Week 8 (October 13): The American Revolution, 1775–1783

Discussion Question 7: Go to Lessons, Course Documents, History Websites, and view the websites on the American Revolution: What did you learn about the American Revolution? Give specific examples.
Readings: Davidson, Chapter 6.
View: American Revolution websites.
Quiz 6: Chapter 6.
Video, PowerPoint or podcast presentation due Sunday October 19.

Week 9 (October 20): The Constitution, 1776–1789

Discussion Question 8: Go to Lessons, Course Documents, Primary Sources, The Constitution, read "The Constitutional Convention Debates the Slave

Trade" and answer the following question: What does the constitutional debate about the slave trade tell us about the nature of the new nation?

Readings: Davidson, Chapter 7 and "The Constitutional Convention Debates the Slave Trade."

Quiz 7: Chapter 7.

Week 10 (October 27): The Early Republic, 1789–1824

Readings: Davidson, Chapters 8 and 9.
Quiz 8: Chapters 8 and 9.
Exam 2: Due Sunday November 2.

Module 3

Week 11 (November 3): The Market Revolution, 1815–1850

Discussion Question 9: Go to Lessons, Course Documents, History Websites, The Market Revolution, and view the websites on European views of America: What did European travelers think of America? Give specific examples.

Readings: Davidson, Chapter 10.
View: European views of America websites.
Quiz 9: Chapter 10.

Week 12 (November 10): Rise of Democracy, 1824–1840

Discussion Question 10: Go to Lessons, Course Documents, Primary Sources, Rise of Democracy, and read the Seneca Falls Declaration. After reading the Seneca Falls Declaration, how democratic do you think the US was during this period?

Readings: Davidson, Chapters 11 and 12 and "Seneca Falls Declaration."
Quiz 10: Chapters 11 and 12.

Week 13 (November 17): Antebellum Slavery, 1820–1860

Discussion Question 11: Go to Lessons, Course Documents, History Websites, Antebellum Slavery, view any two websites on slavery and tell us what you learned.

Readings: Davidson, Chapter 13.
View: Slavery websites.
Quiz 11: Chapter 13.

Week 14 (November 24): Westward Expansion 1820–1850

Discussion Questions 12: Go to Lessons, Course Documents, PowerPoint Presentations, Westward Expansion, and view the painting *American*

Progress by John Gast: After viewing *American Progress* by John Gast, describe what you see and tell us what the main message or viewpoint of the painting is. What does the word "Progress" mean here? Give specific examples.

Readings: Davidson, Chapter 14.

View: *American Progress* by John Gast PowerPoint presentation.

Quiz 12: Chapter 14.

Week 15 (December 1): The Coming of the Civil War, 1850–1861

Discussion Question 13: Go to Lessons, Course Documents, Primary Sources, The Civil War, read the documents and answer the following questions: Why did the southern states secede from the United States? Was it because of slavery, states' rights, or was it for some other reason?

Readings: Davidson, Chapters 15, "The South Reacts to Lincoln's Election," "A Declaration of the Causes which Impel the State of Texas . . .," "Declaration of the Immediate Causes which Induce and Justify . . .," "Declaration of the Causes of Secession, Georgia," and "Declaration of the Immediate Causes Which Induce and Justify the Secession of South Carolina . . ."

Quiz 13: Chapter 15.

Local history paper due Sunday December 7.

Extra credit paper due Sunday December 7.

Week 16 (December 8): The Civil War, 1861–1865

Readings: Davidson, Chapter 16.

Quiz 14: Chapter 16.

Final exam due Tuesday December 16.

The syllabus is adapted from the model syllabus of the Distance Education departments at Joliet Junior College.

Website review guide

Students spend much of their time on this course, and in other courses, examining websites for information. Some of these websites are very well produced and some are not. Students need to develop critical perspectives on websites and assess how convincingly the website presents information. Students can review a website in much the same way as they can review a book. This guide will help students to determine what makes a reliable or unreliable website and what are the strengths and weaknesses of a particular site.

Description of website

What period and subject does the website cover? What is the purpose of the website? Is it an archive of primary sources, a teaching resource, or a presentation by a historian? Who is the intended audience? Is the intended audience researchers, college students or others? Does the website contain primary sources? Are there obvious sources missing? Does it contain enough information about its subject and include enough resources?

Viewpoint of the website

Who are the authors of the website and what credentials do they have? Are they credible? A professor of British history at a well-known university would seem to have the necessary credentials for a website devoted to the British Empire, for example. What is the viewpoint of the site? Is the site biased toward one viewpoint or another? Does it exclude certain sources or facts that would throw doubt on the viewpoint? Who is sponsoring the site? A facist party website on the Holocaust or a Ku Klux Klan website on Martin Luther King, for example, would suggest obvious bias. A labor union website, or Chamber of Commerce website, devoted to industrial relations may also warrant extra inspection. Examine the web address, or URL, to help determine the credibility of a website. An URL ending in "edu" refers to an educational institution, "org" to an organization, "com" to a commercial organization, "gov" to a government institution and "net" to a network. A domain name ending in "edu" would seem to suggest strong credentials for a history website. Overall, is the site historically accurate?

Technology and design

Discuss the design of the website and the ease of navigation. Is the site user-friendly? Does the site make effective use of technology? Is the site interactive? Does it contain games or simulations? Does it make use of audio and video? When was the website last updated? Do the links work? Are the links relevant and appropriate for the site? Comment on the visuals of the site. Is there too much text and not enough visuals? Do the font and colors make the website inviting to viewers? Do the graphics serve a function or are they visual gimmicks?

What do you think is the greatest strength of the website and the greatest weakness?

For an example, see the review of the *Learning Curve: The Great War* website (designed by the Public Record Office, the National Archives in Great Britain) on the Public History Resource Center website at www.publichistory. org/reviews/View_Review.asp?DBID=78 (January 2004).

Consent for participation in oral history project form

You are being asked to be a subject in a research paper for a World History Since 1500 class conducted by _____ a student at Joliet Junior College. We ask that you read this form and ask any questions you may have before agreeing to be in the project.

Your participation in this project is voluntary. Your decision whether or not to participate will not affect your current or future relations with the College.

Why is this research study being done?

I am a student in a World History Since 1500 class at Joliet Junior College and as part of the course requirement I am required to write a paper on the role of a family member in recent world history. I want to audio tape an interview with you and use your answers as information for my paper. Eventually, the tape will be deposited at the Joliet Area Historical Society archive.

What procedures are involved?

I want to interview you as part of my research. I will ask you a series of questions, which I will tape and use as information for my paper. You will be required to sign this consent form. The interview will not be tape-recorded until the signed consent form is given to the interviewer.

What are the potential risks and discomforts?

The only possible risks are that you may be embarrassed by my questions or that you may tell me something that you later regret. These risks are minimal because you can tell me that you want to provide me with information "off the record" and I will shut off the tape recorder. Moreover, you can call me subsequent to the interview, and before the paper and tape are deposited in the archive, and instruct me to delete information I taped that you now would prefer to keep private.

Are there benefits to taking part in the study?

While there are no direct short-term benefits to you by participating in this study, the long-term benefit will be that a history of your family will be documented.

What about privacy and confidentiality?

The audio tape of our interview will be kept securely by me and you can have access to the audio tape to verify any information. The tape will then be given to Dr John Lyons, history instructor at Joliet Junior College. Eventually, the tape will be deposited at a public archive such as the Joliet Area Historical Society.

Will I be reimbursed for any of my expenses or paid for my participation in this study?

No, you will not be paid or receive any gifts for participating in this study.

Can I withdraw or be removed from the study?

You can choose whether to be in this study or not. You may also refuse to answer any questions you don't want to answer and still remain in the study. The interviewer may withdraw you from this research if circumstances arise that warrant doing so. By agreeing to be interviewed for this study, the interviewer is under no obligation to include the information you provide in the study.

Who should I contact if I have questions?

The researcher conducting this study is _____. You may ask any questions you have now. If you have questions later, you may contact the researcher at: Phone: _____ You may also contact my advisor, Dr John Lyons, at 815 280 2742.

Remember: Your participation in this research is voluntary. Your decision whether or not to participate will not affect your current or future relations with the College

You will be given a copy of this form for your information and to keep for your records.

Signature of subject or legally authorized representative

I have read (or someone has read to me) the above information. I have been given an opportunity to ask questions and my questions have been answered to my satisfaction. I have been given a copy of this form. I agree to participate in this study, and to have my tape recording deposited in a public archive.

_____   _____
SIGNATURE   DATE

_____   _____
PRINTED NAME

_____   _____
SIGNATURE OF RESEARCHER   DATE (must be same as subject's)

Group project website review rubric

Category	Excellent	Good	Average	Poor	Fail
Group analysis and interpretation	The group analyzed the website in depth and applied the criteria in the rubric. The group demonstrated clarity of argument, depth of insight into the topic and clear evidence of critical thinking. 10 pts	The group analyzed the website and applied the criteria in the rubric. The group demonstrated good critical thinking but could be improved with more analysis and creative thought. 8–9 pts	The group analyzed the website but did not apply the criteria in the rubric. The group demonstrated some critical thinking but could be improved with more analysis and creative thought. 6–7 pts	The group analyzed the website, but did not make good use of the rubric. The group demonstrated poorly developed critical thinking. 4–5 pts	The group did not analyze the website and did not use the rubric. The group demonstrated no real critical thinking. 0–3 pts
Group writing skills	Standard English syntax and grammar were used. 5 pts	Few, if any, errors in syntax or grammar. 4 pts	Some errors with syntax and grammar. 3 pts	Many problems with syntax and grammar. 2 pts	Poor syntax and grammar were used. 0–1 pts
Group collaboration	The group maintained excellent communication throughout. Group members worked as a group not as individuals. Final report represented a cohesive analysis of the website. 5 pts	The group maintained good communication throughout. Most group members worked as a group not as individuals. Final report represented a cohesive analysis of the website. 4 pts	Some members maintained communication but others did not. Some group members worked as a group but others contributed as individuals. Final report did not represent a cohesive analysis of the website. 3 pts	Some members maintained a minimal amount of communication; others did not. Members worked primarily as individuals. Final report did not represent the view of the total group. 2 pts	Very little communication among group members. Members worked as individuals. Some did not contribute at all. Final report represented the views of one or two members of the group. 0–1 pts
Individual contribution	Shared some excellent ideas with the group, assumed a role with the group, that benefited the group, and strived for progress and consensus. 80 pts	Shared good ideas with the group, assumed a role that somewhat benefited the group, and strived for progress and consensus. 64–79 pts	Shared some ideas with the group, role in the group a little unclear, and sometimes strived for progress and consensus. 48–63 pts	Occasionally shared ideas with the group, did not assume an active role, and did not actively support group progress and consensus. 32–47 pts	Rarely shared ideas with the group, did not play any role in the group, and did not support group progress and consensus. 0–31 pts

Discussion board rubric

Category	Excellent	Good	Poor
Analysis and interpretation	In a minimum 250-word posting, provides excellent ideas that stimulate discussion. Postings are characterized by clarity of argument, depth of insight into the topic and clear evidence of critical thinking. 6 pts	Good ideas that sometimes stimulate discussion. Good critical thinking but could be improved with more analysis and creative thought. 3–5 pts	Poorly developed ideas that do not add to discussion. Poorly developed critical thinking. 2 pts
Evidence	Arguments are well supported by referring to the readings/sources. 3 pts	Readings/sources are not used enough. 1–2 pts	No use of the readings/sources. 0 pts
Response to other students	Responds thoughtfully at least twice to other students in paragraph-length postings. 4 pts	Responds once to other students in a paragraph-length posting. 2 pts	Does not respond to other students. 0 pts
Writing skills	Standard English syntax and grammar were used. 2 pts	Some problems with syntax and grammar. 1 pt	Poor syntax and grammar were used. 0 pts

Peer assessment rubric

Purpose: Students can come to understand the characteristics of quality work by assessing the work of others. We can also improve our own work by having others thoughtfully examine it.

Process: Read each of the essays provided by others in your group. Look at the Essay Rubric below and grade the essay according to the categories laid out in the rubric. In one paragraph, explain what you liked about the essay and in another paragraph explain what can be done to improve the essay. Return the graded essay with the comments to the student and the instructor. The student may revise the essay in light of your comments and then submit the final paper to the instructor.

Remember: Don't use hurtful language or criticize your peers' work unnecessarily. We want constructive criticism not unnecessary criticism. Being overly critical of other students' work will not impress the instructor. Provide the sort of constructive feedback you would like your paper to receive.

Grade: I will grade your peer evaluation out of ten points and the grade you provided for each of your peers' essays will comprise 10 percent of their overall grade.

Category	Excellent	Good	Average	Poor or Fail	Grade
Introduction and conclusion	First paragraph sets the context for the paper. Thesis is evident and points to be argued well stated. Conclusion summarizes the main points of the essay. 9–10 pts	Thesis is not entirely apparent but the essay context is evident. Conclusion summarizes most of the main points of the essay. 7–8 pts	First paragraph does not set the context of the paper. Thesis is hidden among many sentences and hard to piece together. Conclusion summarizes some of the main points of the essay. 6 pts	Thesis is not apparent nor is the context of the essay. Conclusion does not summarize the main points of the essay. 0–5 pts	
Evidence	All facts presented in the essay are accurate and relate back to the thesis. 27–30 pts	Almost all facts presented in the essay are accurate and occasionally relate back to the thesis. 23–26 pts	Most facts presented in the essay are accurate but the evidence presented does not prove the thesis. 18–22 pts	There are several factual errors in the essay. There is no real effort to present evidence to back up the thesis. 0–17 pts	
Structure and organization	The essay is very well organized. One idea follows another in a logical sequence with clear transitions. 18–20 pts	The essay is pretty well organized. One idea may seem out of place. Clear transitions are used. 16–17 pts	The essay is a little hard to follow. The transitions are sometimes not clear. 12–15 pts	Ideas seem to be randomly arranged. 0–11 pts	
Analysis	The entire essay answers the assigned question in a sophisticated way. Topic sentences relate to the question and the main idea of the paragraph. 27–30 pts	Most of the essay is related to the assigned question. Most of the topic sentences relate to the question and the main idea of the paragraph. 23–26 pts	Some of the essay is related to the assigned question. Some of the topic sentences relate to the question and the main idea of the paragraph. 18–22 pts	No attempt has been made to relate the essay to the assigned question. None of the topic sentences relate to the question or to the main idea of the paragraph. 0–17 pts	
Writing skills	The essay has no spelling, punctuation or grammar errors. Clear paragraph construction is used with strong topic sentences and one main idea per paragraph. 9–10 pts	The essay has fewer than three writing errors. Clear paragraph construction is mostly used. 7–8 pts	The essay has four or five writing errors. Clear paragraph construction is sometimes used. 6 pts	The essay has more than five writing errors. Clear paragraph construction is never used. 0–5 pts	

Course evaluation form

Answer each of the questions below. Please submit your responses to the Distance Education department before the end of the semester:

1 What did you think of the textbook?

2 What did you think of the oral history paper assignment?

3 What did you think of the exams?

4 What did you think of the quizzes?

5 Which discussion board question/assignment did you like the most and which did you like the least?

6 Which assignment did you like the most and which did you like the least?

7 Were the study guides and rubrics clear?

8 What did you most like about the course?

9 What did you least like about the course?

10 How could this course be improved?

Additional resources for teachers

Websites

Center for History and New Media website at http://chnm.gmu.edu/resources/essays/ provides a number of essays on teaching history with new media.

The Center for Teaching History with Technology at http://thwt.org/ aims to help history instructors incorporate technology into their courses. The website provides a whole host of free online resources.

Centre for Learning and Performance Technologies at http://c4lpt.co.uk/index.html is an excellent site for discovering the latest technologies and tools for online learning.

E-learning Conferences Worldwide at www.conferencealerts.com/elearning.htm will keep you up to date with upcoming Internet-based education and educational technology conferences.

H-OEH (Online Education in the Humanities) at www.h-net.org/~oeh/ is a listserv run by H-Net (History-Net).

The Internet Archive at www.archive.org/index.php is building a digital library of Internet sites and other cultural artifacts in digital form.

Learning Times at www.learningtimes.org is a fine website for teachers to keep abreast with developments in online learning. It offers the opportunity to interact with peers from around the world and contains a wealth of information for online teachers.

MERLOT at www.Merlot.org is a searchable collection of online teaching materials.

Online Teaching at http://onlineteaching.ning.com is a website for online teaching practitioners to share ideas about technology and pedagogy.

Stephen's Web at www.downes.ca is hosted by Stephen Downes, one of the foremost authorities on e-learning and the use of blogs, wikis and other social software in education.

Teaching and Learning Conferences Worldwide at www.conferencealerts.com/ school.htm will keep you up to date with upcoming conferences in teaching and learning.

World History Matters at http://worldhistorymatters.org is an online resource for world history instructors.

Journals

History Teacher Every historian who is serious about improving their teaching should read this journal. It contains solid articles and book reviews on both traditional and online teaching.

Journal of Online Learning and Teaching This is an online publication addressing the educational use of multimedia resources.

Innovate is an online journal that focuses on the use of information technology to enhance education.

Online Classroom This journal is full of useful tips for teaching online. It is available in print or online from Magna at www.magnapubs.com.

Teaching History: A Journal of Methods Another journal that contains articles and book reviews to help the history teacher keep abreast of new innovations in teaching.

Podcasts

Blackboard@Palomar at www.palomar.edu/atrc/Bb/Bb.xml: The Academic Technology Department of Palomar College in California takes us through creating a Blackboard course. This podcast is also very informative for those that use CMSs other than Blackboard.

Digital Campus at http://digitalcampus.tv: This podcast is produced by the Center for History and New Media and is not just about online learning but about all aspects of using technology for education.

Learning Times Green Room at www.ltgreenroom.org: This podcast will keep you current with new online teaching tools and methods.

Palomar College Academic Technology Podcasts at www.palomar.edu/atrc/ podcast.xml: Produced by the Academic Technology Department of Palomar College in California, this lively podcast discusses technology in education. Each episode contains tech news, teaching tips and tech reviews. Informative show notes are available at www.palomar.edu/atrc/podcast.xml. Accessed June 15, 2008.

Teaching With Blackboard at www.blackboard.niu.edu/blackboard/resources/ podcast: Produced by the Faculty Development and Instructional Design Center at Northern Illinois University, this podcast offers many tips for teaching online and is not only for the Blackboard user.

Blogs

eLearning Technology at http://elearningtech.blogspot.com: Tony Karrer, CEO of a software, Web and e-learning development firm, provides his views on the latest developments in e-learning.

Lisa's Online Teaching Blog at http://lisahistory.net/wordpress: Lisa Lane, a history instructor at MiraCosta College in California, shares her astute thoughts on teaching online.

TerenceOnline: An eLearning Resource Center at http://terenceonline.blogspot. com: Terence Armentano, the Assistant Director of Online Education at Bowling Green State University, provides a wonderful blog on technology, Web 2.0, e-learning and education.

Notes

1 I. Elaine Allen and Jeff Seaman, *Growing By Degrees: Online Education in the United States* (New York, Alfred P. Sloan Foundation, 2005); I. Elaine Allen and Jeff Seaman, *Making the Grade: Online Education in the United States* (New York, Alfred P. Sloan Foundation, 2006); and I. Elaine Allen and Jeff Seaman, *Online Nation: Five Years of Growth in Online Learning* (New York, Alfred P. Sloan Foundation, 2007).
2 Open University, *Facts & Figures 2005/2006* (Open University, 2006), 1.
3 "Universities Expand E-Learning." Accessed June 14, 2008 at: http://news.bbc.co.uk/2/hi/uk_news/education/4361711.stm.
4 *The Chronicle of High Education* (May 12, 2006), A38.
5 Dennis A. Trinkle, "History and the Computer Revolutions: A Survey of Current Practices," *Journal of the Association for History and Computing* 2 (April 1999).
6 Michael Arnone, "Many Students' Favorite Professors Shun Distance Education," *The Chronicle of Higher Education* (May 10, 2002), A39–40.
7 Jeffrey R. Young, "The 24-Hour Professor," *The Chronicle of Higher Education* (May 31, 2002), A31–33.
8 Ellen Laird, "I'm Your Teacher, Not Your Internet-Service Provider," *The Chronicle of Higher Education* (January 3, 2003): B5.
9 Fall 2005 student evaluation in the possession of the author.
10 RateMyProfessors.com, May 21, 2007.
11 Email from student, May 11, 2006 in the possession of the author.
12 Spring 2004 student evaluation in the possession of the author.
13 I. Elaine Allen, Jeff Seaman and Richard Garrett, *Blending In: The Extent and Promise of Blended Education in the United States* (New York: Alfred P. Sloan, 2006). Accessed June 15, 2008 at: www.sloan-c.org/publications/survey/pdf/Blending_In.pdf 2.

Index